THE
Non GMO
COOKBOOK

THE Non·GMO COOKBOOK

RECIPES AND ADVICE FOR A NON-GMO LIFESTYLE

MEGAN WESTGATE & COURTNEY PINEAU

of the **Non-GMO Project**

Skyhorse Publishing

Skyhorse Publishing books may be purchased in bulk at special discounts for sales promotion, corporate gifts, fund-raising, or educational purposes. Special editions can also be created to specifications. For details, contact the Special Sales Department, Skyhorse Publishing, 307 West 36th Street, 11th Floor, New York, NY 10018 or info@skyhorsepublishing.com.

Skyhorse® and Skyhorse Publishing® are registered trademarks of Skyhorse Publishing, Inc.®, a Delaware corporation.

Visit our website at www.skyhorsepublishing.com.

10 9 8 7 6 5 4 3 2 1

Library of Congress Cataloging-in-Publication Data is available on file.
ISBN: 978-1-62636-084-6

Printed in China

$\mathcal{D}$edicated to the luminous green of sunlight shining through leaves in the garden. To the gentle rain and the pungent promise of dark, rich soil. To the magic of seeds. Dedicated to that deep, insistent song that calls us to be reverent, loving stewards of this one precious Earth.

Contents

Introduction

Every day we hear from people who are concerned about GMOs (genetically modified organisms). As awareness spreads, people from all walks of life are increasingly looking for ways to avoid GMOs in the food they are eating and feeding to their loved ones.

As the directors of the Non-GMO Project, our mission is to preserve and build North America's non-GMO food supply and to provide non-GMO choices to consumers through our product verification program. We believe that everyone has a right to know what's in their food and we are thrilled to be offering this cookbook as a resource for enjoying safe, healthy meals.

Away from the office, we are both passionate about growing and preparing wholesome, delicious food. Together with our families on our respective homesteads in northwest Washington state, we grow as much of our own food as possible. Vegetables from organic seeds and eggs from our chickens—raised on Non-GMO Project Verified feed—are staples in our diets, as are simple ingredients from our local farmers market and food co-op.

This cookbook reflects our non-GMO way of life, and also the choices and values of many other individuals in the non-GMO community. In endeavoring to make this more than a compilation of recipes, we solicited submissions from leaders of the movement—from accomplished speakers and authors to food bloggers and everyday citizens who have taken up the non-GMO mission. Throughout this book, we share their stories along with their recipes and we hope you find them as inspiring as we do.

Our heartfelt wish is that everyone be deeply nourished by the food they eat. With shared commitment and thoughtful choices, we can all enjoy safe, healthy food and protect it for generations to come.

Megan Westgate, Executive Director of the Non-GMO Project
Courtney Pineau, Assistant Director
May 2013

About GMOs

What is a GMO?

Genetically modified organisms (GMOs) are plants or animals created through the process of genetic engineering. This experimental technology forces DNA from one species into a different species. The resulting GMOs are unstable combinations of plant, animal, bacterial, and viral genes that cannot occur in nature or in traditional breeding. To give you an idea of just how weird this can get, in 1991 a variety of tomato was engineered with genes from the Arctic flounder to make it frost-tolerant. Fortunately, that product was never brought to market, but it's a good illustration of how unnatural GMOs are.

Almost all commercial GMOs are engineered to withstand direct application of herbicide and/or to produce an insecticide. Despite biotech industry promises, none of the GMO traits currently on the market offer increased yield, drought tolerance, enhanced nutrition, or any other consumer benefit.

How common are GMOs?

In the United States, GMOs are in as much as 80 percent of conventional processed food.

What are the most common GMOs?

In the Non-GMO Project's Product Verification Program, we have three categories of GMO risk: High, Monitored, and Low.

High-risk crops: These crops are currently in commercial production in genetically engineered form. Contamination risk is high, and ingredients derived from these crops must be tested every time before being used in Non-GMO Project Verified products.

Alfalfa (first planting 2011)
Canola (about 90 percent of US crop)
Corn (about 88 percent of US crop)

Cotton (about 90 percent of US crop)
Papaya (most of Hawaiian crop)
Soy (about 94 percent of US crop)
Sugar Beets (about 95 percent of US crop)
Zucchini and Yellow Summer Squash (about 25,000 acres)

Animal products (milk, meat, eggs, honey, etc.) are also considered high-risk because of contamination in feed.

Monitored crops: The monitored category is for crops where there are suspected or known instances of contamination from GMO relatives or other sources. We test these crops regularly to assess risk and move crops to the "high-risk" category for ongoing testing if we see contamination.

Beta vulgaris (e.g., chard, table beets)
Brassica napus (e.g., rutabaga, Siberian kale)
Brassica rapa (e.g., bok choy, mizuna, Chinese cabbage, turnip, rapini, tatsoi)
Cucurbita (e.g., acorn squash, delicata squash, patty pan)
Flax
Rice
Wheat

Common ingredients derived from GMO risk crops

Amino acids, aspartame, ascorbic acid, sodium ascorbate, vitamin C, citric acid, sodium citrate, ethanol, flavorings ("natural" and "artificial"), high-fructose corn syrup, hydrolyzed vegetable protein, lactic acid, maltodextrins, molasses, monosodium glutamate (MSG), sucrose, textured vegetable protein (TVP), xanthan gum, vitamins, yeast products.

You may also be wondering about . . .

Tomatoes: In 1994, genetically modified Flavr Savr tomatoes became the first commercially produced GMOs. They were brought out of production just a few years later, in 1997, due to problems with flavor and ability to hold up in shipping. There are no

The Community Food Co-Op in Bellingham, Washington, where Megan serves on the board of directors.

genetically engineered tomatoes in commercial production and tomatoes are considered "low-risk" by the Non-GMO Project Standard.

Potatoes: Genetically modified NewLeaf potatoes were introduced by Monsanto in 1996. Due to consumer rejection by several fast-food chains and chip makers, the product was never successful and was discontinued in the spring of 2001. There are no genetically engineered potatoes in commercial production and potatoes are considered "low-risk" by the Non-GMO Project Standard.

Salmon: A company called AquaBounty is currently petitioning the Food and Drug Administration (FDA) to approve its genetically engineered variety of salmon, which has met with fierce consumer resistance.

Pigs: A genetically engineered variety of pig, called Enviropig, was developed by scientists at the University of Guelph, with research starting in 1995 and government approval sought beginning in 2009. In 2012 the University announced an end to the Enviropig program and the pigs were euthanized in June 2012.

Are GMOs safe to eat?

Most developed nations do not consider GMOs to be safe. In fact, in more than sixty countries around the world, including Australia, Japan, and all of the countries in the European Union, there are significant restrictions or outright bans on the production and sale of GMOs. In the United States and Canada, GMOs have been approved based on studies conducted by the same corporations that created them and profit from their sale.

A growing body of evidence connects GMOs with health problems, environmental damage, and violation of farmers' and consumers' rights. At the Non-GMO Project we hear from people on a daily basis who are deeply concerned about the potential impacts of GMOs and are taking matters into their own hands by choosing to opt out of the GMO experiment.

Are GMOs labeled?

Unfortunately, even though polls consistently show that the majority of people want to know if the food they're purchasing contains GMO, at this time the United States and Canada do not require foods containing genetically engineered ingredients to be labeled. In the absence of mandatory labeling, the Non-GMO Project was created to give consumers the informed choice they deserve.

Up until now the powerful biotech lobby has been successful in keeping this critical information from the public; however, there is a growing movement of people demanding the right to know what is in their food. Over the past several years, the Right to Know effort has gained significant momentum throughout the United States and Canada. Through marches, rallies, petitions, social media, and targeted outreach campaigns, consumers are demanding that the government respect their right to know what's in their food by labeling GMOs. In the United States, there are also major state-level campaigns under way focused on GMO labeling legislation. The Non-GMO Project is working in partnership with these campaigns to bring awareness to the importance of consumers' right to know and to support policy change that will help protect the food supply in the future.

Do Americans want non-GMO foods and supplements?

Polls consistently show that a significant majority of North Americans would like to be able to tell if the food they're purchasing contains GMOs (a 2012 Mellman Group poll found that 91 percent of American consumers wanted GMOs labeled). And according to a 2009 CBS/*New York Times* poll, 53 percent of consumers said they would not buy food that has been genetically modified. The Non-GMO Project's seal for verified products gives the public an opportunity to make an informed choice when it comes to GMOs.

What are the impacts of GMOs on the environment?

More than 80 percent of all GMOs grown worldwide are engineered for herbicide tolerance. As a result, use of toxic herbicides like Roundup has increased fifteen times since GMOs were introduced. GMO crops are also responsible for the emergence of "super weeds" and "super bugs," which can only be killed with ever more toxic poisons like 2,4-D (a major ingredient in Agent Orange). GMOs are a direct extension of chemical agriculture and are developed and sold by the world's biggest chemical companies. The long-term impacts of GMOs are unknown, and once released into the environment these novel organisms cannot be recalled.

How do GMOs affect farmers?

Because GMOs are novel life forms, biotechnology companies have been able to obtain patents with which to restrict their use. As a result, the companies that make GMOs now have the power to sue farmers whose fields are contaminated with GMOs, even when it is the result of inevitable drift from neighboring fields. GMOs therefore pose a serious threat

to farmer sovereignty and to the national food security of any country where they are grown, including the United States and Canada.

How can I avoid GMOs?

Choose food and products that are Non-GMO Project Verified! Use the Non-GMO Project website at www.nongmoproject.org, or the Non-GMO Project app to find products that have been verified compliant with the Non-GMO Project's rigorous standard. When Non-GMO Project Verified options are not available, choose Certified Organic products, or low GMO risk alternatives. Throughout the cookbook you will find suggestions on how to avoid GMOs when grocery shopping and cooking; also check out our ingredients substitution chart on page 160.

Can you tell if produce has been genetically engineered by the PLU?

A PLU (price look-up code) is that little number you see on produce stickers. If it's a four-digit number starting with a "4" that tells you the product is conventional. If it's a five-digit number starting with a "9" you can be assured that the item is Certified Organic. Identifying genetically engineered produce, though, is not so easy. Five-digit codes starting with "8" are reserved for GMOs, but the usage is optional and as a result you are unlikely to ever see it in a store (we never have). Funny how biotechnology companies love to talk about how great their products are, but then are so afraid to label them. You would never find an organic farmer who wasn't proud to label their products truthfully! We always look for the "9" when we're buying our fruits and vegetables, and we recommend you do, too.

What is the Non-GMO Project?

The Non-GMO Project is a nonprofit organization committed to preserving and building the non-GMO food supply, educating consumers, and providing verified non-GMO choices. We believe that everyone has a right to know what's in the food they are eating and feeding to their loved ones.

What we do

Our primary strategy for achieving our mission is to leverage the power of the marketplace. If people demand non-GMO products, the market will deliver them. Since 2007, we have been working with food companies, producers, retailers, and consumers to build demand and supply for non-GMO products in the United States and Canada.

Product Verification

The Non-GMO Project operates North America's only third party verification program for GMO avoidance. In order to earn the Non-GMO Project Verified label, a product undergoes a rigorous review process to assess compliance with our highly technical standard. The process usually takes at least a few months, and for high-risk products it includes a facility inspection and the establishment of ongoing testing protocols. Once verified, a product is reevaluated annually. Since our label first appeared in 2010, Non-GMO Project Verified has become the fastest-growing claim in the natural products industry, with more than 10,000 verified products.

Retailer Programs

Our strong relationships with natural food stores are foundational to our strategy for changing the food supply. We offer comprehensive retailer programming, including staff training, pocket guides, in-store signage, and many other tools. In 2010, we founded Non-GMO Month, an October event that has been growing exponentially every year, with more than 1,500 natural food stores participating in 2012.

Public Outreach

Whether we are answering calls or email, public speaking at events, or posting GMO news to social media, there is nothing like experiencing the public's engagement with this issue. Changing the food supply isn't easy. When we're mired in technical challenges or logistical hurdles, it is the energy and support that comes from our interactions with the non-GMO community that inspire us. We love using our social media tools to help cultivate these connections and to grow the non-GMO movement. We're committed to maintaining our Facebook page as the most comprehensive and up-to-date source of GMO news on the web.

Living Non-GMO

To support you on your non-GMO journey, we recently created a community lifestyle website. At www.livingnongmo.com you can access more recipes, instructional videos, expert blogs, and other resources for education and connection. From shopping non-GMO on a budget to tips for eating non-GMO at restaurants, our goal is to help make it fun and easy for you to live non-GMO!

Breakfasts and Beverages

A great way to approach going non-GMO in your home is to start with what you and your family eat for breakfast. A meal-by-meal approach may help make any dietary changes a bit easier for young, picky eaters. Another reason to start with breakfast is that many conventional breakfast cereals and breads contain corn, soy, and canola—all high GMO risk ingredients. These ingredients can also be found in alternative dairy beverages and are the most common components of the feed ingested by dairy cows.

Despite the prevalence of GMOs in the typical breakfast, ensuring this meal is non-GMO is made easy by the abundance of delicious Non-GMO Project Verified breakfast options. This section offers an array of great breakfast choices for all types of diets. You can also find a full list of Verified cereals on the Non-GMO Project's website.

In our homes, we frequently start our day with a fresh juice or smoothie, and then follow this with a grain-based or protein-rich breakfast. In fact, at the Non-GMO Project it is not uncommon to walk through the office in the morning and see mason jars on people's desks filled with fruit and vegetable concoctions of various colors and consistencies. Starting your morning with plenty of fresh produce can be a great way to give your day a nutrition jump-start. Since the only GMO-risk fruit at this time is Hawaiian papaya, smoothies and fresh juice are fantastic non-GMO breakfast options.

Asparagus and Asiago Frittata

Rebecca Spector, Center for Food Safety

Rebecca is West Coast Director at the Center for Food Safety in San Francisco, where she champions policy initiatives at the state and federal level and coordinates public outreach campaigns to promote healthy, safe, and sustainable food systems.

Gluten-free, Vegetarian
Serves 8

8 eggs, beaten

1 cup Asiago cheese, grated (or try crumbled fontina or goat cheese for variety)

1 teaspoon fresh rosemary, finely chopped

1 teaspoon fresh thyme, finely chopped

1½ tablespoons extra virgin olive oil

½ onion, finely chopped

1 bunch asparagus, washed and chopped into 1-inch pieces (do not use ends)

4 garlic cloves, peeled and minced

3 tablespoons balsamic vinegar (optional)

Sea salt and pepper to taste

Preheat oven to 350 degrees.

Whisk eggs and combine with Asiago cheese, rosemary, thyme, ¼ teaspoon salt, and ¼ teaspoon pepper in large mixing bowl and set aside. Heat 1 tablespoon olive oil in skillet. Add the onion and sauté for 5 to 10 minutes over high heat with ¼ teaspoon salt and a few pinches of pepper. Reduce heat to medium, add asparagus, and lightly sauté for 5 minutes. Add garlic and stir lightly for another 5 minutes. Add skillet ingredients into the egg and herb mixture and add additional salt and pepper to taste.

In a 9-inch sauté pan (cast iron preferred), heat the remaining oil to just below the smoking point. Swirl oil around the sides of the pan, turn heat to low, then immediately pour the frittata mixture into the pan. The pan should be hot enough so the eggs sizzle. Cook the frittata over low heat for 2 to 5 minutes, until the sides begin to set. Then transfer to the oven and bake, uncovered, 20 to 25 minutes until the frittata is golden and firm. Remove frittata from oven and let stand for 2 minutes. Loosen the frittata gently with a rubber spatula, place a plate over the pan, flip it over, and gently turn the frittata out. Brush with the vinegar if desired. Cut into wedges and serve.

Baked Eggs and Greens

Katje Cleary-James

In 2002 Katje's father died at age sixty-nine from exposure to the herbicide Agent Orange. This loss spurred Katje to spend her time educating people about GMOs and what they are in the context of their own food supply. Her way of life and healthy eating habits have helped her husband of seventeen years keep his multiple sclerosis at bay without drugs, and her own health issues have diminished as well. She is dedicated to ensuring that her children and grandchildren do not eat GMOs.

Gluten-free
Serves 1

1 tablespoon butter
1 small handful kale or spinach greens, roughly
    chopped
¼ red pepper, diced
2 pieces of no-nitrate bacon, cooked and chopped

2 eggs
2 dashes of Bragg Organic Sprinkle Seasoning
Pinch of sea salt
⅛ cup raw cheese, grated

Put butter and greens in a small ramekin and put in toaster oven at 350 degrees for about 2 minutes. In a small bowl, beat eggs and add seasoning and sea salt. Meanwhile, remove ramekin and add red pepper and bacon. Pour eggs over all ingredients and add the cheese. Bake additional 4 to 5 minutes or until eggs are puffy and set.

Megan collects fresh eggs from her chickens.

Garbanzo Bean Flour Pancakes

Sarah Gordon, Squarebar

Sarah, along with her husband Andrew, is the cofounder of Squarebar, a Non-GMO Project Verified nutrition bar. Their commitment to non-GMO is both personal and professional, and they formulated Squarebar to be completely free of high-risk ingredients like corn and soy.

Dairy-free, Gluten-free, Vegetarian
Serves 4

2 cups garbanzo bean flour

3 teaspoons baking powder

1 teaspoon cinnamon

Pinch of sea salt

2 cups water

2 eggs

¼ cup walnut oil (plus 1 teaspoon to oil the pan)

¼ cup unsweetened applesauce

A few drops of liquid stevia

Preheat oven to 170 degrees, and use oven-safe plate to keep pancakes warm.

Mix dry ingredients together in a medium bowl. Add water and whisk. Add eggs, oil, applesauce, and stevia, and whisk together.

Heat 1 teaspoon of walnut oil in a skillet (cast iron preferred) over medium heat. When pan is hot, drop in pancake batter by the ½ cup. Cook pancakes for about 90 seconds on the first side, then flip and cook for about 60 seconds on the second side. Continue with remaining batter, adding a little oil in between each pancake. Serve topped with coconut nectar, pure maple syrup, or fruit topping of your choice.

Oatmeal Banana Pancakes

Ali Segersten, Whole Life Nutrition

Ali is a mother of five children, author of two gluten-free whole foods cookbooks, and a nutrition educator. Her mission is to empower people with healthy GMO-free recipes, knowledge of whole foods, and cooking skills in order to maintain a healthy, vibrant life and sustainable future.

Dairy-free, Gluten-free, Vegetarian
Serves 3 to 4

2½ cups gluten-free oat flour
1½ teaspoons baking powder
½ teaspoon baking soda
¼ teaspoon sea salt
4 medium ripe bananas

2 large eggs
3 tablespoons melted virgin coconut oil (plus extra for cooking)
1 cup water

Preheat oven to 170 degrees, and use oven-safe plate to keep pancakes warm.

In a medium-sized bowl, whisk together oat flour, baking powder, baking soda, and sea salt.

In a separate mixing bowl, add the ripe bananas and mash with a fork. Then whisk in the eggs, melted coconut oil, and water. Pour the dry ingredients into the wet and whisk together. Sometimes a few tablespoons of extra water are needed if the batter thickens too much during mixing.

Heat a skillet (cast iron preferred) over medium heat until the pan is hot. Add a teaspoon or so of coconut oil to the pan, then drop in pancake batter by the ½ cup. Cook pancakes for about 90 seconds on the first side, then flip and cook for about 60 seconds on the second side. Continue with remaining batter, adding a little coconut oil in between each pancake.

Blueberry Quinoa Spice Breakfast Bowl

Roberta Pescow, Narrow Escape Duo, LLC

Roberta is a jazz singer and a freelance writer. She has been vegetarian for thirty-eight years and cares deeply about the rights of all living beings. She tries to eat as naturally and cruelty-free as possible and is committed to keeping GMOs out of her diet.

Dairy-free, Vegan
Serves 3

½ cup tricolor quinoa, soaked, rinsed and drained
1 cup filtered water
1 small apple, chopped
½ cup blueberries
3 Medjool dates (or 6 Deglet dates), chopped
2 tablespoons raisins
1 teaspoon cinnamon
¼ teaspoon cardamom

⅛ teaspoon ginger
⅛ teaspoon allspice
⅛ teaspoon cloves
2 teaspoons vanilla extract
1 tablespoon chia seeds
1 tablespoon hemp seeds
Plant-based milk (coconut, hemp, almond, rice, etc.)

Place quinoa, water, apple, blueberries, dates, and raisins in a saucepan and bring to a boil. Reduce heat and stir in spices and vanilla. Cover and simmer for about 15 minutes, until quinoa is tender and water is absorbed. Remove from heat. Stir in chia seeds and hemp seeds. Spoon into bowls and top with your favorite plant-based milk. Serve warm. Spices can be adjusted to taste.

Nut Butter and Berry Breakfast Bowl

Ryan Black, Sambazon

Ryan, a surfer who grew up in Southern California, was raised to believe that caring for health and happiness is as important as caring for community and our planet. After falling in love with açaí bowls and other tasty Amazon Superfoods on a surf trip to Brazil in 2000, he started Sambazon, which now offers an array of Non-GMO Project Verified beverages and frozen goodies.

Dairy-free, Gluten-free, Vegetarian
Serves 1

2 Sambazon Original Smoothie Packs
½ banana
⅛ cup apple juice
1 handful blackberries (or any berry)
1 spoonful nut butter

Optional toppings:
¼ to ½ cup granola
5 to 6 blackberries
1 to 2 tablespoons local honey

Let Smoothie Pack defrost for 5 minutes at room temperature. In package, break the Smoothie Pack into smaller pieces, then open and put contents in blender with remaining ingredients. Blend until smooth, then pour into a serving bowl. Top with suggested toppings or whatever you're in the mood for!

Fast & Easy Blueberry Scones

Liisa Winkler, One Management, NYC

Liisa is an international model and a mom. Her children are three and six years old and always ask about where their food comes from. As a family, they are fully committed to eating GMO-free and supporting small farms.

Dairy-free, Vegan
Serves 4

2 cups spelt flour
½ cup coconut sugar
1½ teaspoons baking powder
1 tablespoon cinnamon

1 cup frozen blueberries
¼ cup sunflower oil
½ cup almond milk (or coconut or rice)

Preheat oven to 425 degrees.

In a large bowl, stir together flour, sugar, baking powder, and cinnamon. Stir in blueberries. Add oil and milk and combine with your hands to form a loose dough. Form into a ball while still in the bowl. Pat down to approximately 1 inch thickness and cut into six wedge-shaped pieces. Bake on a cookie sheet for 12 to 15 minutes, until bottoms begin to turn golden brown. Let cool a bit before removing.

Oatmeal Power Muffins

Amber Shea Crawley for Oriya Organics

Chef Amber Shea created this recipe for Oriya Organics. Offering Non-GMO Project Verified plant-based protein powder, Oriya Organics was founded by father/son team Steven and Jonathon Larson after realizing they both suffered from an allergy to dairy products.

Dairy-free, Gluten-free, Vegetarian
Serves 6

1 cup old-fashioned rolled oats
½ cup Oriya Organics Superfood Protein Medley or brown rice protein
½ cup coconut palm sugar (or granulated sweetener of choice)
¼ teaspoon baking soda
Big pinch of sea salt
¼ cup melted coconut oil
2 eggs, room temperature
⅓ cup raisins

Preheat oven to 350 degrees.

In a medium bowl, whisk together oats, Superfood Protein Medley, sugar, baking soda, and salt. Add the melted coconut oil and both eggs and whisk to combine. The batter will be thick. Fold in the raisins.

Divide the batter equally into six cups of a lightly greased muffin tin. Bake for 13 to 14 minutes, until the muffins are puffed and the tops spring back when lightly touched. Let cool completely before eating. Best enjoyed with a smear of nut butter and your favorite jam or jelly!

Megan enjoys baking with wholesome ingredients such as freshly ground spelt, coconut sugar, and eggs from her chickens.

Oak Nut Raw Food Bar

Alicia Funk, Living Wild Project

Alicia Funk is the editor of six books on herbal medicine and the coauthor of the recently published Living Wild: Gardening, Cooking and Healing with Native Plants of California *(FlickerPress, 2013).* She is the founder of The Living Wild Project, *a website with simple recipes for enjoying nutrient-rich, non-GMO sources of truly local food. Alicia lives off the grid with her three children and her husband, Michael, who is a founding board member of the Non-GMO Project.*

Dairy-free, Gluten-free, Vegetarian
Serves 3

3 cups of freshly ground nut meal
    (prepared oak nut, sunflower, or walnut)
½ cup of ground seeds or dried berries
½ cup of seasonal fresh fruit (wild blackberries,
    currants, strawberries, or madrone)

¼ cup honey
¼ cup edible wildflowers, for garnish (optional)

Mix together nut meal, seeds, berries, and fresh fruit; stir until just moist. Flatten the mixture on a plate and drizzle with fresh honey. Slice and serve. Edible wildflowers can be added for a lovely garnish.

To make oak nut flour:

Collecting and cracking acorns can be a fun family activity. All species of oak trees produce edible acorns, but they require a process of soaking in water, called "leaching," to turn them into a usable flour. Collect acorns from the ground in the fall. Keep only the acorns without holes and store in a basket in a warm, dry location (ideally near a wood stove or heater) until spring. Crack with a hammer and remove shells. Remove the red skins by heating nuts at 200 degrees for 10 minutes. Roughly grind nuts (a food processor works well for this) and leach by boiling for about five minutes and then straining through cheesecloth. Use the flour immediately (it'll be more like a dough at this stage) or dry in a food dehydrator or spread on a cookie sheet and bake in your oven at the oven's lowest temperature setting. Two cups of shelled nuts will yield approximately one cup of flour. Oak nut flour is gluten-free and a good source of protein.

Apple Pie Energy Bars

Annemarie Rossi, Real Food Real Deals

In 2012 Annemarie founded Real Food Real Deals, *a blog devoted to helping people feed their families whole foods on a budget. The married mother of two elementary school-aged children, Annemarie is active in the PTA at her children's school. It's a priority for her to educate her children and their peers about the importance of avoiding highly processed food, and she's trying to spread the word to as many people as possible.*

Dairy-free, Gluten-free, Vegan
Serves 8

1½ cups walnuts
1 cup dried apples
1 cup dates

¼ teaspoon cinnamon
⅛ teaspoon ginger
⅛ teaspoon sea salt

In a food processor, combine all the ingredients and chop them until a paste is formed. Don't chop them so much that you can't see little bits of walnuts, apples, and dates. Test to see if the mixture binds together. If not, add a couple more dates.

Transfer the mixture to a 7 x 7-inch pan lined with wax paper. Press down evenly. Refrigerate for at least two hours and then cut it into eight bars. Store them in an airtight container in the refrigerator.

Cinnamon Raisin Granola

Corinne Shindelar, INFRA (Independent Natural Food Retailers Association)

Corinne is the CEO of INFRA, President of the Non-GMO Project Board of Directors, and mother of four. Spending time in the kitchen baking and cooking with her two-year-old granddaughter are her favorite ways to relax, and she is enthusiastic about providing good food habits for the next generation.

Dairy-free, Gluten-free, Vegan
Serves 4

3 cups rolled gluten-free oats
1 cup walnuts, roughly chopped
1 cup raisins
½ cup sunflower seeds
1 tablespoon cinnamon

½ teaspoon sea salt
½ cup safflower oil
½ cup maple syrup
1 teaspoon vanilla extract

Preheat the oven to 350 degrees.

Mix the oats, walnuts, raisins, sunflower seeds, cinnamon, and salt (if desired) together in a large mixing bowl. Make a well and pour in the oil, syrup, and vanilla. Mix together well.

Bake on a cookie sheet for 10 minutes, then flip the granola over and bake an additional 10 to 12 minutes. To flip the granola using two cookies sheets of the same size, lay the second cookie sheet on top of the first, and do a quick flip from one cookie sheet to the other. Mix the granola around on the tray to ensure even browning. Watch the edges as they can brown more quickly than the rest (depending on your oven). Serve as is or with sliced apples.

Megan and Courtney review recipes as they test dishes for the cookbook.

Chocolate Coconut Granola

Kali Orkin, The Conscious Consumer

Kali has been GMO-free since 2008. A culinary school graduate with an MBA in Sustainable Business, Kali blogs at The Conscious Consumer, *helping to educate people on living a lifestyle that is better for their community and the planet.*

Dairy-free, Gluten-free, Vegan
Serves 6

6 cups rolled oats

½ cup coconut oil

½ cup grade B maple syrup

½ cup raw cocoa powder

1 cup pecans, roughly chopped

1 cup shaved coconut, unsweetened

½ cup hemp or chia seeds (optional, but great nutritional boost)

Preheat oven to 325 degrees.

In a large bowl, mix together oats, oil, and syrup. Spread evenly on a large cookie sheet and bake for 20 minutes. Stir, sprinkle on additional ingredients, and bake for 20 more minutes.

Purple, Purple, Green Smoothie

Sandi Rechenmacher, Simply Nutritious

As an organic gardener for the past forty years, Sandi's commitment to non-GMO foods comes naturally to her. For the past ten years she has been passionately involved in teaching nutrition education. Through embracing wholesome plant foods with no GMOs, Sandi has witnessed her health and the health of her family improve, and watched those she teaches who adopt a similar diet feel better as well.

Dairy-free, Gluten-free, Vegan
Serves 2 to 3

2½ cups water
Large handful of greens (spinach,
        collards, kale, chard, or beet greens)
4 to 6 drops liquid stevia or 2 tablespoon
        raw agave
¼ section lemon, peel and all

1 small piece fresh ginger, peel and all
2 oranges, peeled
1 apple, cored
1 banana, peeled
2 cups blueberries (or frozen mixed berries, pine-
        apple, or any other fruit you like)

Blend water (some of this amount can be ice) along with the greens, liquid stevia, lemon, and fresh ginger for about 1 to 2 minutes until smooth. Add fruit and blend again for another minute, until all ingredients are well mixed and the color of the smoothie is uniform throughout.

No-Stress Blood Orange Spritzer

Sonnet, For the Love of Food and Natural Vitality

Sonnet is a certified holistic health coach, food educator, blogger, and writer. She teamed up with Natural Vitality to create this calming spritzer using Natural Vitality's Natural Calm, a Non-GMO Project Verified magnesium supplement.

Dairy-free, Gluten-free, Vegan
Serves 2

2 cups fresh blood orange juice (or about 6 larger oranges, juiced)

1 to 2 teaspoons Natural Calm Raspberry-Lemon Flavor magnesium supplement

16 ounces sparkling water

Ice

Fresh mint for garnish (optional)

Pour orange juice into a large pitcher and mix in magnesium powder. Add sparkling water, ice, and garnish with fresh mint (optional). Serve and enjoy!

Ancient Super Shake

Valeria Baskerville

After losing eighty pounds by switching to a non-GMO lifestyle, Valeria is in the best shape of her life. Her commitment to eating non-GMO foods helps her feel secure about living a long, healthy life.

Dairy-free, Gluten-free, Vegan
Serves 1

16 ounces unsweetened almond milk

3 tablespoons hemp protein powder

2½ tablespoons raw cacao powder

1 teaspoon coconut sugar

Blend all the ingredients until smooth and completely integrated. Serve and enjoy!

Green Lemonade

Carissa Bonham, Creative Green Living

Carissa's blog teaches people about how to make easy greener choices for their families. She has been active in mandatory GMO labeling initiatives in Washington, Oregon, and California. Carissa believes that our right to know if the food we eat is genetically modified is one of the fundamental human rights issues of our time.

Dairy-free, Gluten-free, Vegan
Serves 2

3 small or 2 large lemons
1 cucumber
2 Granny Smith apples

⅓ green bell pepper
5 kale leaves or 2 cups baby spinach

Wash all ingredients thoroughly. Cut away the peel of half of the lemons. Cut produce into pieces appropriate for your juicer. Juice all fruits and veggies together.

Planting a Non-GMO Garden

Outside of cooking and eating non-GMO, one of our favorite ways to help protect and build a non-GMO food supply is through organic gardening. There are so many amazing heirloom and open-pollinated seeds available. Planting and saving non-GMO seeds not only helps to protect the biodiversity of our seed supply, it also helps preserve an important part of our cultural heritage. Many heirloom seeds have an incredible lineage and story connected with them. Plus, they frequently have superior nutrition and taste in comparison to conventional store-bought varieties.

When buying seeds and plant starts for your garden it is important to make sure that they have not been genetically engineered, and that the company you are purchasing from is not developing GMO varieties or purchasing their seeds from biotechnology companies. There are several ways you can do this. First, whenever possible, buy seed that is Non-GMO Project Verified. You can also look for companies that have taken the Safe Seed Pledge. These companies pledge to "not knowingly buy or sell genetically engineered seeds or plants." In many areas of the country there are also small, local seed growers who produce organic seed that is non-GMO. One of the advantages of locally grown seed is that it will be well-adapted to the growing conditions in your area.

If you do not have a home garden, a visit to a local farm or urban garden (if you are in the city)

can be a great way to experience firsthand the importance of a healthy seed supply. It can be a profound experience to look at a tiny carrot seed and realize that it contains all of the information necessary to grow into a beautiful carrot!

Courtney grows a variety of vegetables, flowers, and heirloom beans on her homestead in Bellingham, Washington.

Starters, Sides, and Salads

There is nothing quite as delicious and enlivening as a well-treated vegetable. That may sound silly, but the truth is that vegetables can be the highlight of a meal if they are prepared in a way that showcases their vibrancy. For instance, a beautifully orchestrated fresh salad or a sun-ripened tomato can absolutely delight the taste buds. We hope this section inspires you to explore all of the creative and tasty ways you can prepare vegetables.

Thankfully there are few GMOs found in the produce aisle at this time. GMO tomatoes are no longer being sold—whew! However, you do have to keep an eye out for GMO sweet corn and yellow crookneck squash. At the Non-GMO Project we monitor several types of vegetables, like beets and zucchini, to make sure they don't cross-pollinate with GMO varieties, so your best bet is to buy Non-GMO Project Verified or Certified Organic vegetables whenever possible.

Kale Chips

Robyn O'Brien, AllergyKids

A former financial and food industry analyst, author, Fulbright grant recipient, and mother, Robyn brings insight and detailed analysis to her research on the health of American families and their food systems. Following her career as an equity analyst, Robyn had four children and founded the AllergyKids Foundation, a nonprofit focused on restoring the health of American children. On Mother's Day 2009, Random House published her critically acclaimed book, The Unhealthy Truth: How Our Food Is Making Us Sick—And What We Can Do About It. *Robyn is an advocate for labeling new additives in our food supply—especially those, like GMOs, that weren't in the foods that we ate as kids.*

Dairy-free, Gluten-free, Vegan
Serves 4

1 bunch kale, chopped into bite-size pieces
2 tablespoons extra virgin olive oil
¼ teaspoon sea salt

1 tablespoon lemon juice (optional)
¼ teaspoon cayenne pepper (optional)
¼ teaspoon black pepper (optional)

Preheat oven to 350 degrees.

Place the kale in a large bowl with oil and salt and any optional ingredients you want. With your hands, toss and mix ingredients together. Spread the kale out on a baking sheet. Bake for about 10 to 15 minutes, until kale is dark green and crispy. Cool and serve!

Kale and Quinoa Salad with Cranberries

Tara Cook-Littman, GMO Free CT

Tara is a mother of three young children and is determined to secure a safe and healthy food supply for their future. A former New York City prosecutor and a Certified Holistic Health Counselor, Tara combined her passion for health and wellness with her advocacy skills and is now the Director of GMO Free CT. This grassroots organization is dedicated to educating the citizens of Connecticut about the risks associated with GMOs and how to avoid them. GMO Free CT also has a Right To Know GMO CT campaign to advocate for the passage of a GMO labeling law in Connecticut.

Dairy-free, Gluten-free, Vegetarian
Serves 2 to 4

1 cup quinoa
1 bunch kale
1 cup raw sunflower seeds
1 cup dried cranberries
2 oranges
1 lemon
2 tablespoons honey
⅓ cup extra virgin olive oil
⅓ cup apple cider vinegar

If possible, soak quinoa overnight and drain in the morning. Boil 2 cups of water and add the quinoa. Bring to a simmer and cook for 20 minutes or until water is absorbed.

While the quinoa is cooking, remove leaves of kale from stem and rip into tiny pieces. It is very important that the kale is torn into bite-sized pieces and massaged thoroughly; otherwise the raw kale can be difficult to chew. Put the kale at the bottom of a bowl and pour the hot quinoa directly on top to slightly wilt the leaves. Add the cranberries and sunflower seeds and mix together.

Zest one orange and the lemon, then combine with the juice of both oranges, the juice of the lemon, 2 tablespoons honey, olive oil, and apple cider vinegar. Mix together and pour over the quinoa dish. Mix and serve!

Spinach Apple Salad

Chris Keefe, Non-GMO Project

Food, food, food—its quality, its safety, and its future availability all hang on decisions we make now about what to grow, how we grow it, and how we eat it. As Retailer Programs Manager at the Non-GMO Project, Chris is grateful to be in a position where his work does some good for our food system, our farmers and producers, and the health of future generations. In his spare time, Chris is an avid climber and amateur photographer.

Dairy-free, Gluten-free, Vegan
Serves 1

2 cups spinach, chopped
1 apple, chopped
½ cup raisins
½ cup toasted or roasted almonds (or favorite nuts)

2 tablespoons flaxseed or hempseed oil
Balsamic or sweet vinegar
Pinch of sea salt

Mix the spinach and apples in a salad bowl. Toast nuts in a cast iron pan or roast in the oven at 400 degrees until golden. Add the nuts, raisins, vinegar, and oil to the salad. Mix it all together and enjoy.

Fennel Salad

Carmen Lyman, Carmen Lyman Translations

Carmen lives on Kauai with her husband. They are committed foodies and make all of their meals from scratch, incorporating ingredients from their backyard garden and the eggs of their free-ranging hens. Carmen supports the non-GMO movement because she believes in honesty in food labeling.

Gluten-free, Vegetarian
Serves 2

1 fennel bulb, cored and sliced very thinly, only using the white part
1 handful walnuts, chopped

2 tablespoons Parmesan/Grana cheese, grated
¼ cup extra virgin olive oil
Sea salt and pepper to taste

Toss all ingredients and either serve immediately or chill in the fridge. This is a very hearty salad that will last and improve when chilled over time. Try making it in the morning and serving it for dinner. Fennel is not especially common, so it will surprise guests with its flavor and simplicity.

Traveler's Multi-Purpose Tabouli

Pamm Larry, labelgmos.org

Pamm is the Initial Instigator and Chief Rabble Rouser for Proposition 37. She continues to be the Northern California Director for labelgmos.org, the original grassroots movement in California that laid the groundwork for Proposition 37. A GMO labeling gypsy, Pamm travels frequently throughout California. She likes to cook a large batch of this salad, put it in the cooler, and then dress it up in various ways to enjoy over the course of several days.

Dairy-free, Gluten-free, Vegan
Serves 10 to 12

5 to 7 cups quinoa

Large bunch parsley (curly or Italian), minced

1 to 1½ cups, extra virgin olive oil

Cook the quinoa slightly al dente. Mix the quinoa, parsley, and olive oil; this will serve as the base that can be used with different embellishments. When you are ready to eat, put enough of this base in a bowl for the required servings, then add the optional ingredients listed below. If the tabouli is a bit dry after all the ingredients are added, use a little more olive oil. Mix and serve.

Optional: (per 4 servings)

1 cup zucchini, thinly sliced

1 cup garbanzo, red, or white beans

½ cup cilantro, finely chopped

2 tablespoons lime or lemon juice

1 cup green or red bell peppers, diced

2 tablespoons red onion, minced or thinly sliced

1 cup tomatoes, diced

1 cup jicama, diced or julienned

½ cup carrots, thinly sliced

½ cup celery, thinly sliced

½ cup roasted pepitas

Sea salt and black pepper or chili pepper to taste

½ cup fennel, thinly sliced

Lettuce (romaine, raw spinach, raw chard, arugula, radicchio, or a mix)

Olives (various, to taste)

Roasted nuts (various, to taste)

Cheese (various, to taste)

Curried Freekeh Salad

Bonnie Matthews, Freekeh Foods Brand

Bonnie is the cofounder of Freekeh Foods. Also a Wellness Warrior blogger with the Dr. Oz Show, Bonnie discovered freekeh (an ancient grain) when she was 280 pounds and ready for a lifestyle change. Freekeh became a staple in her diet as she lost 130 pounds. It's her mission to share with people how fitness and delicious, nonprocessed, non-GMO foods can help change our health. This recipe is from her self-published cookbook, 30 Ways to Freekeh!

Dairy-free, Vegan
Serves 6

1 cup cracked freekeh
2½ cups vegetable broth
1 sweet potato or yam, cut into 1-inch cubes
1 large red pepper, diced
½ red onion, diced
4 garlic cloves, peeled and minced
2 tablespoons extra virgin olive oil or grapeseed oil

3 to 5 tablespoons mild curry powder
½ cup dried cranberries or raisins
1 cup apricots, chopped
1 cup frozen peas, thawed
1 cup sliced almonds or pepita seeds
Sea salt and pepper to taste

Preheat the oven to 375 degrees.

Pour 2½ cups of broth and the freekeh in a saucepan and bring to a boil for 1 minute. Reduce heat to low, cover, and simmer for about 25 minutes until the freekeh is tender. Once the freekeh is cooked, place in a separate dish to cool in the refrigerator.

Place sweet potato cubes on a foil-lined baking sheet and drizzle a little olive oil on them. Bake for about 25 minutes or until tender. Remove from oven and set aside.

In a large skillet, heat oil over medium heat and toss in red pepper, onion, and garlic. Cook for 3 to 5 minutes and then add curry powder, salt, and pepper. Cook until the onions are translucent. Set aside to cool. Toss freekeh in bowl with vegetable mixture, add dried fruits, nuts, peas, and sweet potatoes. Season to taste and serve. Try adding lightly steamed broccoli, sautéed cauliflower, chickpeas, or lentils to this recipe.

Simple Soba Salad

Maureen Kirkpatrick, The Big Carrot

Maureen is a member of The Big Carrot, a worker-owned natural food co-op in Toronto that has been leading the way for thirty years and is Ontario's first certified Organic retailer and Vegetarian Deli. The Big Carrot is proud to be one of the founding members of the Non-GMO Project. Maureen currently serves on its Board of Directors. This is one of Maureen's favorite non-GMO dishes from fellow member and Big Carrot Executive Chef John Robertson.

Dairy-free, Gluten-free, Vegan
Serves 2 to 3

12 ounces soba noodles

3 green onions, thinly sliced

¾ teaspoon sesame oil

2 tablespoons sesame seeds

2 tablespoons ginger

2 tablespoons mirin

3 tablespoons orange juice, freshly squeezed

6 tablespoons tamari

Pinch of sea salt

Bring 12 cups of water to a boil and add a pinch of sea salt. Add noodles; when they are al dente rinse with cold water and strain.

In a large bowl, stir together green onions, sesame oil, sesame seeds, ginger, mirin, orange juice, and tamari. Add the soba noodles and enjoy!

Tofu-Mushroom Arugula Salad with Caramelized Onions

Mateo Boucher, Real Food Company

Mateo Boucher joined Real Food Company in 2012 with the purpose of transitioning its deli and catering operations to serve all organic, non-GMO, and house-made food. His passion for excellent food and his shared vision with the family-owned store has won rave reviews.

Dairy-free, Gluten-free, Vegan
Serves 4 to 5

2 large yellow onions, thinly sliced
½ pound crimini mushrooms, quartered
12 ounces firm tofu, diced
¼ cup safflower oil (or other high-heat oil)
¼ cup tamari

¼ cup sesame oil
½ teaspoon sea salt
¼ teaspoon black pepper
¼ pound baby arugula
Several sprigs fresh marjoram, chopped

Preheat oven to 375 degrees.

Sauté onions in a portion of the safflower oil, on medium heat, until onions become translucent and begin to brown. Add salt and pepper while cooking. Remove onions from heat and place on a parchment-lined tray or glass dish in a thin layer to cool quickly.

Toss mushrooms in a bowl with a portion of the sesame oil and tamari. Add sea salt and black pepper to taste. Sauté on medium heat until browned and very tender. Set aside to cool.

Toss tofu with a portion of the sesame oil, tamari, and safflower oil. Place on parchment-lined tray or glass baking dish. Roast in the oven with fan on until tofu becomes slightly crispy. Remove from heat and allow to cool.

Combine onions, mushrooms, and tofu in a bowl. Add remaining sesame oil and tamari. Fold in baby arugula and marjoram.

Chicken Summer Salad

Tracy DiTolla, Oakland, New Jersey Farmers Market

Tracy has a cooking blog where she encourages eating healthy, organic foods and shares occasional indulgent recipes made with organic ingredients. She is also the Vice President of the farmers market in Oakland, New Jersey, where they promote organic and non-GMO foods.

Gluten-free
Serves 4

2 cooked chicken breasts, cubed

2 bunches baby kale (or arugula, baby romaine, fresh spinach), roughly chopped

1 peach, sliced

1 small cucumber, peeled and chopped

¼ cup goat cheese crumbles

1 tablespoon plus 1 teaspoon extra virgin olive oil

1 teaspoon balsamic vinegar

Salted pecans to taste

Sea salt and pepper to taste

While the chicken is still warm, mix all ingredients together in a large bowl. Make sure everything is evenly combined and let it sit a few minutes so the goat cheese melts into the olive oil and the kale wilts slightly from the warm chicken. Low-calorie and very healthy, this is a great dish to throw together for a potluck or to serve at any summer party!

Wild Summer Salad

Grant Lundberg, Lundberg Family Farms

Grant is CEO of Lundberg Family Farms, the nation's leading producer of organic and eco-farmed rice and rice products. He is a member of the third generation of the Lundberg family, who have owned and operated the rice farming and processing business in California's Sacramento Valley since it was founded by his grandparents in 1937. An outspoken advocate of non-GMO farming, Grant Lundberg was one of the founding board members of the Non-GMO Project and served on the Board of Directors from 2007 to 2013. He was cochair of the California Right to Know Campaign, which supported labeling of foods containing GMOs.

Dairy-free, Gluten-free, Vegan
Serves 4

1 cup Lundberg Wild Blend rice
¾ cup tomato, seeded and diced
¾ cup green onions, chopped
⅓ cup cooked green peas
4 tablespoons rice vinegar

1 tablespoon sesame oil
1 clove garlic, peeled and minced
½ teaspoon dried tarragon
½ teaspoon sea salt
½ teaspoon black pepper

Cook the rice according to the package directions. Combine cooked, cooled rice with all ingredients. Toss lightly. Chill and serve.

For a non-vegetarian version, try adding 1 cup cooked and cubed chicken breast.

KimChi with Pickled Vegetable Spears

Noah Westgate

Cultivation and preparation of vibrant, healthy food is at the heart of Noah's life mission to create healing for humans and the Earth. A permaculturist and massage therapist, Noah helps fuel the Non-GMO movement by feeding his wife Megan, Executive Director of the Non-GMO Project, an abundance of nourishing foods, including lots of raw salads and ferments.

Dairy-free, Gluten-free, Vegan

2 medium or 1 very large head of Napa Cabbage, coarsely chopped

5 to 10 fresh carrots, sliced in rounds up to ½ inch thick

2 to 3 large daikon radishes, sliced in rounds up to ½ inch thick

1 medium-large fresh ginger root, finely chopped

1 to 10 fresh jalapeño or other spicy peppers, finely diced (to desired spice level)

1 to 10 teaspoons dry crushed red pepper (choose your own spice level)

1 to 10 medium/large cloves of garlic, peeled and minced (optional)

4 tablespoons sea salt

4 cups fresh/filtered nonchlorinated water

Note: The above ingredient list is for basic kimchi. Nearly any firm, fresh vegetable that is in season and abundant can be packed and pickled within it.

Other supplies:

Large crock pot

Glass lid or strong ceramic plate that fits inside of the top half of the crock pot

Breathable cotton dish towel or cheesecloth

Heavy rubber band large enough to fit tightly around the top of the crock pot

Weight to press the kimchi, such as a clean, nonporous stone or a mason jar full of water

> Note: All supplies should be clean and sterile. Never substitute plastic or metal for anything that touches the brine during fermentation.

Make the brine by mixing the salt and water until completely dissolved. Make more or less brine depending on the volume of vegetables.

Mix all vegetables thoroughly, adding peppers and garlic to taste (be aware that a lot of the spiciness is absorbed and mellows out during fermentation). Pack the mixture into a crock and add a cupful of brine at a time. Using a pestle, briefly mash and press the vegetables until they are submerged. Mashing helps them soften, release juices, and absorb the brine.

Press with a ceramic plate or glass lid that is as close a fit to the inside crock diameter as possible, until the veggies are compacted beneath the brine (add more brine if necessary to submerge). Weight the plate if necessary with a full mason jar or other object (don't leave anything plastic or metal in the liquid however). Cover with a kitchen towel or cheesecloth secured with a large rubber band to keep dust and flies and light out but so that it can still breathe.

Let ferment for several days to several weeks depending on how you want it (as it sits the vegetables will soften and the beneficial probiotics will multiply); you can uncover and remove some for sampling along the way (return it to its submerged state when finished). Remove and dispose of anything that grows on top of the water; as long as there aren't air pockets none of this can grow in the submerged veggies. After a week to 10 days it can be moved to the fridge (fermentation speed increases with warmer temperature and slows when cooled).

Pack finished kimchi into glass jars and fill to top with brine. This will last for a very long time in the fridge, especially if the veggies are kept submerged under the brine between uses.

Focaccia with Roma Tomatoes and Onions

Karielyn Tillman, The Healthy Family and Home

Karielyn is a wife and a mother of three. Her website, The Healthy Family and Home, *features and promotes organic, nutrient-dense, healthy, vegan, and raw food recipes and products. She encourages everyone, no matter what diet plan they follow, to read ingredient labels and learn about what is in the foods they eat, to avoid GMOs, and to buy organic or Non-GMO Project Verified whenever possible. Her website motto is "Eat like it matters . . . because it does!"*

Dairy-free, Vegan
Serves 4

1 packet active dry yeast

1 cup warm water (distilled or purified)

1 teaspoon turbinado, or other unrefined sugar (or raw honey for non-vegan)

2½ cups unbleached all-purpose flour

1 teaspoon pink Himalayan salt

¼ cup extra virgin olive oil (to mix into the dough)

2 tablespoons extra virgin olive oil (to drizzle into holes in dough)

1 onion, thinly sliced

2 to 3 Roma tomatoes, sliced

2 to 3 sprigs fresh rosemary, needles removed from the stem

2 tablespoons extra virgin olive oil (to drizzle over the toppings)

In a medium bowl, mix yeast, warm water, and sugar (or honey). Let the mixture rest for about 10 minutes until the yeast "blooms" and bubbles form on the top. Add in the flour, salt, and ¼ cup of olive oil and stir until evenly combined. Turn the dough onto a well-floured surface and knead gently until the dough is smooth, approximately 5 to 10 minutes. Place in a lightly oiled bowl and cover with a kitchen towel. Let the dough rest in a warm place (or a dehydrator set at 100 degrees) until it doubles in size, approximately 1 hour.

Remove the dough from the bowl and press down into a lightly oiled 9 x 13-inch baking sheet until it touches the edges (or divide between two 6-inch cake pans for a

thicker version). Using your fingers, poke holes all over the dough. Drizzle the other 2 tablespoons of olive oil over the dough and into the holes. Preheat the oven to 450 degrees. Let the dough rest until it becomes puffy, about 20 minutes.

Place the onion, Roma tomatoes, and rosemary on top of the dough. Drizzle the toppings with 2 tablespoons of olive oil. Bake for 20 minutes or until golden brown. Remove from oven and cool on rack before serving.

Dean's Own Homemade Corn Bread

Dean Nelson, Dean's Natural Food Market

Dean Nelson opened the original Dean's Natural Food Market in 1995 in Ocean, New Jersey. Its mission statement is to "provide the best organic products available, and to put customer and community before profits." Dean's passion for the natural food industry is second only to his love for family. The ability to contribute to the wellness of his community, and the acknowledgement received from customers and peers that "Dean's does it right" is humbling and inspiring. Dean's Natural Food Market is a proud and ardent supporter of the Non-GMO Project and their mission to educate the public on the issue of GMOs in our food supply.

Vegetarian
Serves 8

2 cups Hodgson Mill yellow corn meal
2 cups Hodgson Mill white flour
1 cup Wholesome Sweeteners light brown sugar
1½ tablespoons baking powder
½ tablespoon sea salt
⅙ tablespoon freshly ground black pepper

⅔ cup frozen sweet corn
2 large eggs
2 cups whole milk
16 ounces sour cream (or vegan alternative)
1 cup unsalted butter

Preheat oven to 375 degrees (325 degrees if convection oven, with fan on).

Line and grease two 9 x 13-inch quarter-sheet pans. In a large bowl, sift together the dry ingredients. Add frozen corn to dry ingredients and mix to coat the corn.

In a separate bowl, beat the eggs and then add the milk and sour cream. Mix well. Melt the butter and stir it into the wet ingredients. Mix together the dry ingredients and liquid ingredients, stirring to eliminate any lumps. Spread batter on pans and bake for 30 minutes, rotating once.

Spinach Puffs

Isabel VanDerslice, Non-GMO Project

Isabel spent her senior year of high school living with a family just outside of Barcelona, Spain, and fell in love with Catalan and Spanish languages, cultures, and especially cooking. While getting her degree in Molecular Biology, she ran several electoral campaigns in Washington State. As the Outreach Coordinator for the Non-GMO Project, Isabel is passionate about protecting our non-GMO food supply. At home, she loves organic gardening and inventing recipes.

Vegetarian
Serves 10

20 ounces fresh spinach, finely chopped

2 cloves garlic, peeled and minced

2 cups herb stuffing mix (or bread crumbs and
    savory herbs)

1 large onion, finely chopped

½ cup Parmesan cheese, grated

⅓ cup butter, melted

4 eggs, well beaten

1 teaspoon pepper

½ teaspoon thyme

½ teaspoon basil

Preheat oven to 350 degrees.

Steam the sliced spinach, allow it to cool, and squeeze out as much liquid as possible. Add remaining ingredients and stir. The mixture should be lumpy and begin to stick together. Shape into small balls about 1½ inches in diameter (it may take a good squeeze) and place on a baking sheet. Not much space is needed between them, as they will not expand.

Bake for 20 minutes or until golden on top and hot all the way through. Serve hot or freeze and reheat for later use.

Spinach-Kale-Mushroom Mashed Potatoes

Allie Oliver-Burns, PoseManikin

Allie is a simple girl from Upstate New York whose blog, PoseManikin, *features her enjoyment of cooking, nature, recycling, robots, music, technology, photography, fashion, and design. Allie is committed to helping spread the word about the incredible benefits of eating food the way nature intended—without GMOs.*

Gluten-free, Vegetarian
Serves 6

5 medium potatoes, cubed	Dash of turmeric
1 cup shiitake mushrooms, chopped	Dash of basil
2 tablespoons butter	Dash of garlic salt
⅓ cup cream	1½ cups kale, chopped
⅓ cup sour cream	2 cups spinach, chopped
Dash of sea salt	Fresh cilantro

Boil potatoes with a dash of sea salt until soft. While potatoes are cooking, sauté shiitake mushrooms over medium heat until lightly browned, about 5 to 10 minutes.

Drain water from potatoes and return potatoes to pan. On low heat, mix in butter, cream, sour cream, turmeric, basil, and garlic salt. Once well mixed, add the kale, sautéed mushrooms, and spinach and stir until the greens are wilted. Heat until warm throughout and serve right away, garnished with cilantro. This goes well with sliced zucchini and carrots sautéed in extra virgin olive oil.

Zesty Guacamole

Alison Levitt, M.D., Doctor In The Kitchen

Alison has always been passionate about eating well and being healthy. She knows that the ultimate recipe for optimal health and longevity is to eat healthily. Alison's company, Doctor In The Kitchen, is committed to making Non-GMO Project Verified products. Alison strongly believes that it is our right to know what is in our food and that it is vital to our health and the health of the planet that our food be clean, natural, and free of genetic modification.

Dairy-free, Gluten-free, Vegan
Serves 6

4 avocados, mashed

Juice of two limes

3 garlic cloves, peeled and minced

4 green onions, thinly sliced

½ red onion, finely chopped

1 teaspoon ground cumin

1 jalapeño, diced

Sea salt and pepper to taste

Mix the mashed avocado with lime juice and then stir in garlic, onions, cumin, and jalapeño. For a healthy twist, serve with Flackers flaxseed crackers.

Lilacs adorn a
farm stand in Port
Townshend, Washington.

Morselicious Bean-Nutty Paté

Maura (Mo) Knowles, Mac-n-Mo's Inc.

Mo the Morselist, a.k.a. Maura Knowles, is a Board Certified Health Coach (AADP), recipe developer, and the creator and CEO of Mac-n-Mo's. She started this vegan, gluten-free, no sodium, no sweeteners, non-GMO baked goods company for her dad, Mac, a diabetic, after he underwent quadruple bypass surgery in 2010.

Dairy-free, Gluten-free, Vegan
Serves 4

¼ cup flax seeds
2 tablespoons flaxseed meal
1 cup water
⅓ cup walnuts

⅓ cup cooked cannellini beans (or beans of choice)
1 clove garlic, peeled
Juice from half a lemon
Black pepper to taste

Combine ¼ cup flax seeds and 2 tablespoons flaxseed meal with 1 cup water. Let it sit for 3 minutes. Combine all ingredients in a food processor or high-speed blender. Blend until smooth and serve chilled.

Soups

Soups are a fantastic way to eat well even when life is busy—which, for us, is pretty much all the time! A big pot of soup made over the weekend offers nourishing dinners for a couple of days, and is also a great grab-and-go lunch for the office. Most of the soups that follow are complete meals unto themselves, and many pair nicely with the starters, sides, and salads in the previous section.

Soups are a generally low GMO risk category of food, especially when made using fresh produce and bulk legumes and grains. One thing to watch out for, though, is sweet corn, which is commonly genetically engineered. If you buy corn from a local farmer, ask them if they are using GMO seeds. At the grocery store, look for Non-GMO Project Verified or Certified Organic options. The same goes for animals products. For more about sourcing non-GMO meat and dairy, see page 102.

Cuban Black Bean Soup

Hannah Kullberg, The Better Bean Company

Hannah first learned about GMOs when she chose this controversial topic for a middle school website-design class back in 2000. The next year, Oregon had a GMO labeling bill on the ballot—Hannah got involved in the campaign and remembers being devastated when it lost after a misleading last minute TV ad campaign by the opposition. Now she's grateful to have a Non-GMO Verified Product out on the market and plans to leverage her status as a small food business owner to support new mandatory labeling efforts in Oregon.

Gluten-free, Vegan
Serves 4

1 tablespoon extra virgin olive oil

1 cup onion, finely chopped

1 large clove garlic, minced

1 medium sweet garnet yam, cubed

1¾ cups water or vegetable broth

1 container (14 ounces) Better Bean Cuban Black
Beans (or cooked black beans)

1 teaspoon coriander (optional)

1 teaspoon oregano (optional)

4 large Swiss chard leaves and stems, chopped

1 tablespoon maple syrup

Sea salt and freshly ground black pepper

In a medium saucepan, heat the oil over medium heat. Add the onions and sauté until brown, stirring frequently, roughly 5 minutes. Add the optional spices and garlic and cook until fragrant, about 1 minute. Add the yam and sauté until soft. Add the water or broth and Better Bean Cuban Black Beans and bring to a boil over medium-high heat. Add the chard, stir to combine, cover, and simmer until the chard is tender, about 10 minutes more. Add maple syrup, salt, and pepper to taste.

Creamy Carrot with a Kick Soup

Liana Shanti, The Rawganic Life

Liana promotes the non-GMO lifestyle on her RawganicVegan Facebook page, providing helpful information on how people can diligently avoid GMO products. With strong advocacy roots, she supports local efforts in Hawaii to fight GMOs and is truly committed to keeping food pure—for everyone.

Gluten-free, Vegan
Serves 4

3 cups carrots, shredded

½ cup tomato, chopped

¼ cup onion, diced

½ cup red bell pepper, diced

1½ cups water or coconut water

¼ cup macadamia nuts (or substitute cashews or almonds)

¼ cup coconut meat (fresh or dried unsweetened)

4 teaspoons date paste (or 2 Medjool dates, pitted)

2 teaspoons mustard

1 teaspoon smoked paprika

1 teaspoon fresh dill

1 teaspoon fresh parsley

½ teaspoon garlic powder

¼ teaspoon chipotle powder (or to taste)

Add all the ingredients to a blender. Blend until smooth and warm, about 2 minutes.

Orange and Avocado Gazpacho

Mary Papoulias-Platis, California Greek Girl Blog

Mary was raised in a Greek community, cooking at home with the finest ingredients. She lived with farmers and growers who worked hard days to provide for the community, and she is passionate about shopping at her local farmers market. She currently teaches culinary classes with a commitment to serve and educate about quality food to everyone.

Gluten-free, Vegan
Serves 6

6 fresh tomatoes, diced (about 4 cups)
2 medium red bell peppers, diced (about 2 cups)
2 cucumbers, peeled, seeded, and diced
½ small sweet onion, minced
2 medium garlic cloves, peeled and minced
⅓ cup red wine vinegar
2 teaspoons sea salt
¼ teaspoon pepper

5 cups tomato juice
1 cup water
1 teaspoon Bragg's Liquid Amino Acids
2 teaspoons fresh Greek oregano, minced
2 teaspoons fresh Greek basil, minced
2 avocados, thinly sliced
2 oranges, peeled and sectioned
Extra virgin olive oil

Combine the tomatoes, red peppers, cucumbers, onion, garlic, vinegar, salt, and pepper in a large glass bowl. Allow to sit for 10 to 15 minutes. Stir in tomato juice, water, amino acids, oregano, and basil. Cover and refrigerate for 3 hours or up to 2 days. Before serving, top with a thin slice of avocado and orange. Drizzle with extra virgin olive oil.

Wild Rice Mushroom Bisque

Michael Potter, Eden Foods

Michael is the Chairman and President of Eden Foods, which has had a non-GMO policy since 1993. With more than forty years in the natural food industry, Michael is a founding board member of the Non-GMO Project, and Eden Foods currently has 173 Non-GMO Project Verified products. He resides in Ann Arbor, Michigan, near his six children (two daughters, four sons) and three grandchildren.

Vegan
Serves 6

6 cups water or soup stock
⅔ cup Eden Wild Rice, soaked, rinsed and drained
1 tablespoon Eden Extra Virgin Olive Oil
1 cup shallots, minced
1 cup baby portabella mushrooms, thinly sliced
½ cup button mushrooms, thinly sliced
2 teaspoons fresh thyme leaves, finely chopped

½ teaspoon freshly ground black pepper, or to taste
2 tablespoons maple syrup
1 teaspoon Eden Sea Salt, or to taste
¼ cup unbleached white flour
2 cups Edensoy Unsweetened soy milk
¼ cup finely chopped fresh chives, for garnish

Place the water, wild rice, and olive oil in a medium pot. Cover and bring to a boil. Reduce the heat to medium-low and simmer about 25 minutes. Add the shallots, mushrooms, and thyme. Cover and simmer another 10 minutes or until the rice is tender. Reduce the heat to low.

Place the pepper, syrup, salt, flour, and Edensoy in a small mixing bowl and whisk until the flour is dissolved. Add the whisked mixture to the soup and stir frequently just until the soup thickens, about 5 minutes. Do not boil. Adjust the salt and pepper seasoning, if desired. Remove and serve garnished with chives.

Celeriac Potato Soup

Dianna Parish, Mobius Builders LLC

Dianna is an interior designer/green contractor who loves to cook healthy, beautiful food. She believes all food should have health as first priority—for people, animals, and the planet—and sees GMO food as being in direct conflict with that.

Gluten-free, Vegetarian
Serves 5

½ cup (1 stick) butter
½ cup extra virgin olive oil
Several sprigs fresh thyme
4 cloves garlic, minced
½ sweet onion, chopped
1 stalk celery, chopped
1 large celery root, peeled and chopped
4 cups baby potatoes (such as Dutch Yellow), cubed

2 fresh chili peppers (such as Serrano for hot; milder varieties also good), minced
2 cups cognac
1 cup shiitake mushrooms, sliced
1 apple, diced
Water or broth
Sea salt to taste

Place ½ stick butter, olive oil, and thyme in heavy soup pot. Simmer on low to melt butter. Add the garlic, onion, and celery to the pot. Simmer until vegetables begin to soften. Add celery root, potatoes, and chili peppers. Seeds can be left in the peppers for a spicier soup, or remove seeds to make it milder. Sauté, stirring regularly until all vegetables are soft. Add 1½ cups cognac and simmer until nearly all liquid disappears.

In a separate skillet, melt ½ stick butter and add shiitake mushrooms and apple. Sauté until both begin to brown. Add ½ cup cognac to mushroom/apple pan and sauté until nearly all liquid is absorbed. Remove mushrooms and apples and set aside to garnish the soup. If any butter or liquid remains in pan, add it to the vegetable pot. Remove thyme sprigs (many leaves will have fallen off). Ladle celery/potato mixture into the blender and purée until smooth. You may add water or broth for desired consistency and for ease of blending. Salt to taste.

Serve hot with warmed mushroom/apples over the top as garnish.

Mommom's Healing Chicken Rice Soup

Joyce McCarus, Lalahjoy Designs

Joyce comes from a long line of home gardeners and cooks. She believes in bringing creativity and color into all of her endeavors, from food and gardening to handmade clothes and accessories. As an artisan, Joyce understands the importance of knowing the source and maker of a product, which is why she is passionate about high-quality local foods and cooking from scratch. She also feels strongly that we must protect our seed supply from the dangers of GMOs, so that future generations can enjoy the same diversity of plants and foods that are available to us now. Joyce loves gardening with her daughter Courtney, the Assistant Director at the Non-GMO Project, by her side.

Dairy-free, Gluten-free
Serves 5

1 large whole chicken
1 tablespoon apple cider vinegar
4 stalks celery with leaves, diced
4 carrots, diced
1 tablespoon extra virgin olive oil
2 medium sweet onions, diced
1 bunch fresh parsley, stems removed, chopped

3 garlic cloves, peeled and minced
1 tablespoon dried thyme
1 can (16 ounces) whole tomatoes, chopped
1 cup long grain brown rice
1 tablespoon sea salt
2 teaspoons pepper
1 lemon

Place whole washed chicken in an 8-quart pot and cover completely with water. Add apple cider vinegar. Bring water to boil and skim off fat from the top. Cover and simmer for 1½ hours.

Sauté onion, celery, and carrots in olive oil over medium heat for 10 minutes. Put aside all vegetables. Strain chicken broth into another 8-quart pot and let chicken cool. Add vegetables to the broth, salt to taste, pepper, and thyme. Strain the juice from whole tomatoes, cut tomatoes into cubes, and add to broth. Add rice. Pull chicken meat from bones and add to broth. Simmer soup for 1½ hours.

To serve, add salt and pepper to taste, and add a squeeze of lemon to each bowl.

Easy Asian Noodle Soup

Misako Binford, San-J International Inc.

Misako is in charge of purchasing ingredients for San-J, a brewer of premium Tamari soy sauce. San-J has always been dedicated to providing highest standards of ingredient purity and is proud to have Non-GMO Project Verified products. Food is a big part of Misako's life, and she loves to cook for friends and family, using ingredients from her own garden. In Japan, her mother taught her that "you are what you eat," and so now she feels lucky for the lesson and the time spent together over lovingly prepared meals. It has become her passion to pass those values down to her daughter and children in the community.

Dairy-free, Gluten-free
Serves 4 to 6

5 shiitake mushrooms, de-stemmed and sliced

4 green onions, thinly sliced

6 cups gluten-free chicken broth

3 tablespoons San-J Gluten Free Tamari

8 ounces maifun thin rice noodles

1 sheet nori seaweed

In a medium saucepan, combine chicken broth, mushrooms, green onions, and San-J Gluten Free Tamari. Bring to a boil. Reduce the heat and simmer on medium-low for 10 minutes.

Cook maifun thin noodles according to the package instructions and drain. Add noodles to the soup. Cut nori sheet into 1-inch strips and sprinkle over the noodle soup before serving.

The Ultimate Tom Yum Soup

Erica Benes, Sol Cuisine

Erica is the Marketing Coordinator for Sol Cuisine, where she has developed a passion for food and food-related topics. Erica believes that making conscious, educated choices about diet is especially important when faced with an industry that can be saturated with skewed and inaccurate information. She is committed to GMO labeling because it promotes a level of transparency that safeguards our future and that of generations to come.

Gluten-Free, Vegan
Serves 4 to 6

6 cups boiled water

1½ cups coconut milk

3 pieces lemongrass, stalks removed and diced

1½ tablespoons fresh ginger or galangal, very thinly sliced

2½ tablespoons sweet and sour chili paste of choice

1½ cups oyster mushrooms, diced

1 onion, diced

1 small tomato, diced

½ cup red pepper, diced

½ cup yellow pepper, diced

1 cup bamboo shoots

2 cups mei qing choi (a mini bok choy hybrid)

1½ cups Sol Cuisine firm tofu, cubed

Garnishes: cilantro, Thai basil, green onion, lime, chili peppers, and bean sprouts

In a large pot, mix water, coconut milk, lemongrass, and ginger. Bring to boil on medium-high heat, and then simmer on low for 15 minutes. Add in sweet and sour chili paste and stir, checking for desired consistency. Throw in oyster mushrooms, onion, tomato, peppers, bamboo shoots, mei qing choi, and tofu. Simmer on low until veggies soften, about 20 minutes.

Remove lemongrass and ginger when ready to serve (optional but recommended especially for lemongrass). Serve each bowl with a side of fresh bean sprouts, Thai basil, cilantro, green onion, a lime wedge, and chili pepper.

Sweet Corn Chowder

Aube Giroux, Kitchen Vignettes Blog

Aube is a documentary filmmaker and award-winning food blogger. She is currently working on a documentary about GMOs and also trying to build awareness with short cooking videos on her blog. She loves to eat, cook, and grow her own food, and she believes that meals are more enjoyable when we know the story behind them.

Gluten-free
Serves 4 to 6

4 ears sweet corn

4 slices bacon (or 2 tablespoons butter), finely chopped

1 medium onion, diced

2 stalks celery, diced

1 small bunch fresh thyme (about 15 sprigs)

2 tablespoons chives or green onion, finely chopped

4 cups chicken or vegetable broth

¼ cup cornmeal or corn flour

2 cups potatoes (new potatoes are best), chopped

1 canned (or dried and rehydrated) chipotle chili, finely chopped (optional)

2 cups half and half

1 teaspoon smoked paprika

Sea salt and pepper to taste

Using a sharp knife, slice corn kernels from the ears of corn; set the kernels aside. In a medium stockpot over medium heat, cook the bacon, stirring occasionally, until the fat is rendered. Add the onion and cook, stirring occasionally, for 5 minutes. Stir in the celery, half of the thyme leaves, and chives and cook, stirring occasionally, for 3 minutes.

Stir in the broth and bring to a boil. Reduce the heat to a simmer. Transfer ½ cup of the liquid to a medium bowl. Add the cornmeal to the bowl, whisking until smooth. Stir the cornmeal mixture back into the chowder. Stir in the potatoes and chipotle (start with one-half of the chopped chipotle and add more if desired, to taste). Cook 10 minutes and then stir in the corn kernels. Cook until the potatoes are tender, 10 to 15 minutes. Reduce the heat to low. Stir in the cream and paprika and cook until just heated through, about 2 minutes. (After the cream is added, do not allow the chowder to boil.) Add salt and pepper to taste. Garnish with sprigs of thyme or chives and serve with warm, crusty bread.

Tomato Bacon Soup

Davina Stuart

Davina is a stay-at-home wife and mom, living in semirural Alaska. Since going gluten-free two years ago, she has become much more aware of what she puts in her body and now also tries to help her family and friends learn how food can affect our health.

Dairy-free, Gluten-free
Serves 6

2 quarts diced, seeded tomatoes (fresh or bottled)
6 green onions, finely chopped
1 small green pepper, diced
½ small onion, diced
6 strips uncured bacon (pork, turkey, or both),
    roughly chopped
Basil, garlic, oregano, and thyme to taste

Sea salt and pepper to taste
Optional toppings:
Mushrooms, sautéed
Onion, chopped
Tomato, diced
Sour cream

Place everything except the bacon into a large pot and cook over medium heat. If using fresh tomatoes, you may need to add a little bit of liquid (stock or a good cooking wine adds a nice flavor). Let this come to a boil, then reduce to a simmer and reduce by about a third to a half, depending on how much liquid you had to start.

Allow to cool slightly and run it through your blender or food processor; purée until smooth. Return to the pot.

While the tomatoes are reducing, chop your bacon into rough pieces and fry until just crispy. Reserve a small amount of cooked bacon as a topping for the soup. Add the rest of the bacon and, if desired, the bacon drippings, to the tomato purée. Return to simmer and allow flavors to come together. Add salt and pepper to taste.

Let soup sit for 10 minutes before serving. Top with bacon, and any other desired toppings.

GMOs and Animal Products

Much of the GMO corn and soy grown in North America is fed to animals, as is some of the canola and cotton. For those who choose to include dairy, eggs, meat, and other animal products in their diet, it is therefore important to know about the animals' feed.

We both keep small flocks of chickens and are lucky enough that the first Non-GMO Project Verified feed company (Scratch and Peck) just happens to be based nearby. Before we had access to feed that had actually been tested for GMOs, we chose blends that were free of corn and soy. We also make sure our chickens' diets are supplemented with plenty of forage from the land around our homes.

If you are buying animal products from the store, look for the Non-GMO Project label or choose Certified Organic products. Organic products aren't tested for GMOs, but genetic engineering is an excluded method under the National Organic Program.

We also recommend using animal products sparingly and consciously. Both of us have spent long periods of our lives being vegan or vegetarian, and while we both include some animal products in our diets now, we do so in moderation and with great reverence.

Megan carries a basket of fresh eggs from the chickens she and her husband raise.

certified organic
Cherry Belle
radish
$2.50
Four Dharma Ridge Farm

certified organic
Easter Egg
radish
$2.50
Four Dharma Ridge Farm

certified organic
Arugula $2.50
with flowers
Four Dharma Ridge Farm

Organically Grown

Main Dishes

From fresh, raw meals to hearty baked dishes, this section has something for every palate and season. In the summer, we like to eat lighter foods like the spring rolls and raw beet ravioli that follow. In the winter, casseroles and occasional meat bring a welcome balance to the cold, wet days.

Fish can be a nice choice at any time of year, and living in the Pacific Northwest, salmon is of course a cherished food. We are watching with alarm as the FDA disregards 1.8 million signatures and moves to deregulate a variety of genetically engineered salmon that grows twice as fast as its traditional counterpart and would devastate wild populations if released. In the future, it will be important to look for the Non-GMO Project Verified label in order to avoid this experimental food. Also, let your grocers know that you don't want GMO fish!

We the people have incredible power. If we stop eating GMO food, producers will stop making it. So remember to communicate your non-GMO preference to your favorite food companies and local food stores. We have often seen major changes in sourcing come about because of a few simple phone calls from concerned consumers.

Beans and Spinach Stuffed Acorn Squash

Leigh Garofalow, Green-4-U Blog

Leigh is mother of two children under the age of four and an environmental blogger and activist. She wants to see our food supply protected from GMOs and to be able to feed her children food that is natural and healthy. When she cooks at home she tries to use 100 percent real food that she knows is natural and GMO-free, which she feels is one of the most important things she can do to keep her kids healthy. Leigh wrote and worked hard trying to get Proposition 37 passed in California and continues to work to keep the public informed on the issues with GMOs.

Vegan
Serves 8

2 acorn squashes

3 tablespoons extra virgin olive oil

1 onion, diced

2 cloves garlic, minced

3 tablespoons tomato paste

4 tablespoons water

1 bunch spinach, chopped

1½ cups homemade cooked white beans

3 tablespoons minced capers, or minced marinated artichoke hearts

Coarse, plain whole wheat bread crumbs

Sea salt and pepper to taste

Preheat oven to 375 degrees. Cut the squash in half. Cut a small portion of the bottom part of each piece so it will stay flat on the plate. Scoop out the seeds and a little bit of the squash to make a small bowl. Then bake the squash for 30 minutes or until soft.

Heat some olive oil in a medium-sized pot and sauté the onions for 3 to 5 minutes until they turn clear. Add garlic about halfway through. Then add the tomato paste and water and stir until completely mixed (if the filling gets too dry, extra oil can be used). Add the spinach and cook until reduced down. Add the beans and capers and heat until fully cooked and hot.

Take the acorn squash halves out of the oven and brush the insides with a little bit of olive oil. Then spoon the bean and spinach mixture into the bowls. Fill them to a heaping, but not overflowing, level. Mix the breadcrumbs and 3 tablespoons olive oil in a bowl. Put the bread crumb mixture on top of the squash halves and put in the broiler on high for 3 minutes or until golden brown and a little crispy. Serve this with a salad with balsamic or Italian dressing.

Stuffed Tomatoes with Pesto and Orzo

Robynn Shrader, NCGA (National Cooperative Grocers Association)

Robynn is the CEO of the National Cooperative Grocers Association (NCGA), which represents 134 food co-ops operating more than 170 stores throughout the United States with over 1.3 million consumer-owners. The NCGA offers all consumers information about what's in our food, where it comes from, where to find great food, how to prepare it, and more. This recipe is an original from the Co+op Stronger Together culinary team, which works closely with co-op staff and other contributors around the country.

Vegetarian
Serves 8

8 medium to large ripe tomatoes
1 package orzo pasta (8 ounces)
2 tablespoons extra virgin olive oil
1 lemon, juice and zest
¼ cup fresh basil, finely chopped
1 cup fresh spinach, finely chopped

2 tablespoons pine nuts, toasted
1 teaspoon garlic, minced
¼ cup grated Parmesan cheese
½ teaspoon sea salt
¼ teaspoon ground black pepper

Cook the orzo according to the package directions, drain well, and refrigerate until cold. In a food processor, blend the pesto ingredients: olive oil, basil, spinach, pine nuts, garlic, and ¼ cup grated Parmesan cheese. In a large bowl, mix together the chilled orzo, pesto, lemon zest and juice, salt, and pepper.

Wash and core the tomatoes, then scoop out the seeds and some of the flesh to make space for the orzo mixture. Slice a small section from the bottom of the tomato so it will sit upright. Fill each of the tomatoes with a few tablespoons of the orzo mixture, sprinkle with shredded Parmesan, and serve at room temperature or chilled.

Accompanied with hummus, baba ghanouj, and toasted pita triangles, these stuffed tomatoes make a lovely alfresco lunch. If you prefer, bake stuffed tomatoes for 15 minutes at 425 degrees and serve warm.

Mexican Lasagna

Jimbo Someck, Jimbo's . . . *Naturally!*

Jim (Jimbo) Someck has been in the natural foods industry since 1973. In 1984 he opened his first store and has since opened up four more stores, all in San Diego. Jimbo joined the Non-GMO Project's Retailer Advisory Board in 2010 and that same year pioneered the first Non-GMO Month. Jimbo's non-GMO product policies, instituted in 2011, serve as a model for retailers across North America. Jimbo is married and has four children. His passion for both organics and non-GMO food is inspired by dedication to his family and to protecting safe food for future generations.

Gluten-free, Vegan
Serves 8

2 cups dried pinto beans, soaked overnight and cooked, or 4 cups of canned beans
2 cloves garlic, chopped
1 tablespoon extra virgin olive oil
1 medium to large yellow onion, diced
1 jalapeño pepper, minced
1½ cups fresh or frozen sweet corn

3 cups water
2 tablespoons tomato paste
1 teaspoon sea salt
1 large bunch fresh cilantro, chopped
1 package corn tortillas
1 cup ground meat, sautéed (optional)
½ cup cheese, grated (optional)

Preheat oven to 350 degrees.

Sauté two cloves of garlic in a tablespoon of olive oil on a medium-low flame. After a few minutes, add the onion and jalapeño. When the onion is translucent, stir in corn. Add water, tomato paste, pinto beans, and salt and bring to a low simmer. Once the mixture is back to a low simmer, add cilantro and remove from heat.

To put the lasagna together, layer corn tortillas on the bottom of a 12 x 9-inch baking pan. You will need to cut some of the tortillas to fit into corners or around circular edges. Once the bottom is covered, scoop the bean mixture over the tortillas until they are completely covered. Add meat and cheese if desired. Place another layer of tortillas on top, cutting them as needed—some overlap is fine. Add another layer of bean sauce over the tortillas to complete your lasagna. Cover with aluminum foil and bake for about 25 minutes so that the tortillas can absorb the liquid from the sauce and become soft.

Vegetarian Baked Ziti

Sarah Christie, Peace Love Organic Mom

Sarah is committed and passionate about the non-GMO movement because she does not want her daughters (ages ten months and seven years) to be raised eating food that is not pure. She buys and feeds her family only organic food and her family has a garden in their backyard that her girls help with. Sarah created a blog called Peace Love Organic Mom *as a resource to help new parents live a natural and organic lifestyle.*

Vegetarian
Serves 4 to 6

16 ounces ziti pasta
6 mushrooms, sliced
16 ounces fresh spinach
3 cloves garlic, chopped
1 can (14.5 ounces) diced tomatoes, drained
16 ounces ricotta

8 ounces mozzarella cheese, grated
8 ounces Parmesan cheese, grated
1 jar (24 ounces) tomato sauce
Extra virgin olive oil
Dash of sea salt

Preheat oven to 350 degrees.

Bring large pot of water to a strong boil. Add a dash of salt and 1 tablespoon olive oil to water. Add pasta to water and boil until pasta is al dente.

While pasta is boiling, add mushrooms, spinach, and garlic to a skillet with 2 to 3 tablespoons olive oil. Sauté until spinach is completely wilted and mushrooms are tender. Mix in diced tomatoes.

Mix ricotta cheese with mozzarella in a large bowl until thoroughly blended. Drain pasta and pour into 13 x 9-inch baking dish. Stir vegetable mixture into pasta. Once vegetable mixture is blended into pasta, add cheese mixture and stir well. Add tomato sauce. Sprinkle Parmesan cheese to evenly cover whole dish. Bake for 30 minutes or until sides are bubbling and top is nicely browned.

Rich and Fragrant Tomato Sauce

Wenonah Hauter, Food & Water Watch

Wenonah Hauter is the Executive Director of Food & Water Watch. She has worked extensively on food, water, energy, and environmental issues at the national, state, and local level. Her book Foodopoly: The Battle Over the Future of Food and Farming in America *examines the corporate consolidation and control of our food system and what it means for farmers and consumers. When tomatoes are in season, Wenonah makes time in her busy schedule to can tomatoes and prepare this tasty sauce. Her favorite tomato is the Olpaca, a delicious heirloom variety that is long like a pepper and has meaty flesh with few seeds.*

Dairy-free, Gluten-free, Vegetarian
Makes 2 quarts

4 pounds fresh tomatoes
5 garlic bulbs, separated, peeled, and pressed
1¼ cups extra virgin olive oil
½ teaspoon honey (or more depending on the
    acidity of the tomatoes)

1 teaspoon salt
1 handful basil, chopped

Dip the tomatoes in boiling water; after they cool, slip off the skins and core. Use a potato masher or your hands to crush them in a large pan.

Sauté the garlic in olive oil. Add the tomatoes, honey, and salt and simmer until the sauce becomes thick and reduces by about half. Depending on the type of tomato this takes 1 to 2 hours. Stir in basil just before serving.

Crispy Baked Fish

Mary Waldner, Mary's Gone Crackers

Mary is the cofounder and chairman of Mary's Gone Crackers, manufacturers of certified organic, gluten-free, and Non-GMO Project Verified crackers, pretzels, cookies, and crumbs. Ensuring that Mary's Gone Crackers products are non-GMO has always been essential for Mary, and she is fully committed to making delicious foods that are based on whole, organic ingredients from the earth's bounty.

Gluten-free
Serves 6 to 8

2 pounds fish
2 cups Mary's Original Seed Crackers with Caraway
½ cup Parmesan cheese, grated
1 tablespoon garlic powder

2 eggs, beaten
Extra virgin olive oil
Dash of sea salt and pepper

Preheat oven to 350 degrees.

Trim excess fat and skin off fish. Pat dry. Crush crackers into crumbs and mix with Parmesan cheese, garlic powder, salt and pepper. Coat fish thoroughly with crumbs, then dip fish in beaten egg mixture and roll it in the crumb mixture again. Place the fish in lightly oiled baking dish. Bake 25 to 30 minutes.

Salmon with Pomegranate-Blackcurrant Sauce

Kristine Kidd, Crofter's Organic

Los Angeles-based chef and author Kristine Kidd loves experimenting with the latest ingredients and finding fresh sustainable foods at local farmers' markets. As Bon Appétit *magazine's Food Editor for twenty years, Kristine expanded upon her lifelong love of food and enjoyed sharing her finds and ideas with readers. Kristine has worked with Crofter's Organic to develop recipes for their Non-GMO Project Verified fruit spreads.*

Dairy-free, Gluten-free
Serves 4

4 wild salmon fillets, 5 to 6 ounces each
1 tablespoon extra virgin olive oil, plus more as needed
Coarse kosher salt and freshly ground pepper
2 tablespoons shallot, minced

½ cup Crofter's Europe Superfruit Spread
⅓ cup dry white wine
3 tablespoons water
2 teaspoons fresh thyme, minced

Preheat the oven to 400 degrees.

Brush the flesh of the salmon with olive oil and sprinkle with salt and pepper. Oil a rimmed baking sheet. Heat 1 tablespoon olive oil in a large nonstick skillet over medium-high heat. Add the salmon (skin side down) and cook until starting to brown on the bottom, about 3 minutes.

Transfer the salmon onto the baking sheet, reserving the drippings in the skillet. Roast the salmon until it feels springy to the touch and is just opaque in the center when cut into with a small sharp knife, about 8 minutes. Remove from the oven and keep warm on the baking sheet.

Warm the reserved skillet over medium heat. Add the shallot and sauté 30 seconds to soften slightly. Mix in the fruit spread, wine, and water. Simmer until the fruit spread dissolves and the sauce thickens slightly, stirring constantly, about 2 minutes. Remove from heat. Mix in the thyme and season to taste with salt and pepper. Divide the fish among four warmed plates. Drizzle the sauce over the fish and serve.

Sprouted Black Bean Burgers

Dudley Evenson, Soundings of the Planet

Dudley and her husband Dean Evenson founded their record label, Soundings of the Planet, in 1979 and produce award-winning healing world music and videos. In addition to their music and media, they are avid gardeners and are in the process of building a 40-foot-diameter geodesic biodome in the field next to their home to grow food year-round.

Dairy-free, Gluten-free, Vegetarian
Serves 8

½ cup dried black beans
1 cup quinoa, soaked, rinsed and drained
½ cup carrots, finely chopped
½ cup zucchini, finely chopped
¼ cup onions, diced

1 cup ground flaxseed
Savory herbs to taste
Sea salt and pepper to taste
1 egg (optional)

Pour a half cup of black beans into a jar and let it sit overnight in water. The next day, pour out the water using a screen or a strainer to catch the beans. Every day, rinse the beans and strain off the water. In a few short days the beans will have sprouted. In a medium saucepan, combine sprouted beans with 2 cups water and cook until beans are soft; strain off excess water and set aside.

In a medium saucepan, combine 2 cups of water with the quinoa. Bring to boil and then turn off; let sit covered for 30 minutes.

Preheat the oven to 400 degrees.

Pour the quinoa into a large bowl and mix in the carrots, zucchini, and onions. Mix in sprouted beans, stir, and season with herbs or sea salt. Add in flax flour to create the consistency to form into a patty. If you like, add in an egg for more cohesion. Form into patties like cookies and place on oiled baking sheet. Bake for about 20 minutes, then turn over once. Alternatively, cook on the stovetop in an oiled frying pan, turning them over several times. Eat as a stand-alone snack or like a burger with all the toppings. These are great to take to potlucks.

Quinoa Cakes

Amela Keric

Amela recently made a commitment to eating a gluten-free diet and purchasing only non-GMO products. For her, health comes first and spending a few extra bucks now costs a lot less in the long run than paying hospital bills later.

Gluten-free, Vegetarian
Serves 4

1 cup quinoa, soaked, rinsed and drained

2 cups water

½ cup mushrooms, roughly chopped

½ cup sun-dried tomatoes

½ cup red or yellow peppers, roughly chopped

½ cup zucchini, roughly chopped (optional)

1 red onion, roughly chopped

1 clove garlic

2 large eggs

2 tablespoons Parmesan cheese, grated

Extra virgin olive oil

Gluten-free bread crumbs

Sea salt and black pepper to taste

Cayenne pepper, dry chives, and/or dried basil to taste

2 tablespoons dijon mustard

2 tablespoons mayonnaise

Boil 2 cups of water and add the quinoa. Bring to a simmer and cook for 20 minutes or until water is absorbed.

While quinoa is cooling, put all of the veggies in a food processor and blend until finely diced, but not to the point where the vegetables begin to purée. Sauté the chopped veggies in a skillet for a few minutes until golden brown. In a medium bowl, mix quinoa, veggies, eggs, and cheese. Form into patties. In a small bowl, combine bread crumbs, salt and pepper and herbs. Lightly coat each patty with olive oil and dip in bread crumb mixture. Place quinoa cakes in oiled skillet and cook for 3 to 5 minutes per side, until golden brown.

To make the dijon dip, mix together the mustard with the mayonnaise and add black pepper to taste. Enjoy!

Buckwheat Soba Noodles with Peanut Sauce

Stacy Weinberg Dieve, Rooted Health

Stacy is the cochair of MOMS Advocating Sustainability, a San Francisco Bay Area-based organization committed to creating healthy communities for children by reducing their exposure to household and environmental toxins, which include GMOs. Stacy strives to feed her family only non-GMO foods and to support both the farmers and companies that are committed to GMO-free ingredients.

Gluten-free, Vegetarian
Serves 2

5 tablespoons peanut butter

¼ cup tomatoes, diced

¼ cup water

1 clove garlic, peeled

2 tablespoons apple cider vinegar

1 tablespoon honey

1 tablespoon tamari

2 teaspoons lemon juice

1 teaspoon ginger powder

1 package buckwheat soba noodles

2 carrots, grated

Place all ingredients except for soba noodles and carrots in a blender or food processor and purée until smooth. Cook soba noodles according to package directions. Stir peanut sauce into the noodles and top with carrots. Extra sauce can be stored in the refrigerator for up to one week.

Thai Red Curry

Cathy Christiansen, Silk

Cathy Christiansen has been Silk's chef for seven years. She's a classically trained pastry chef who turned to Silk when looking for more natural, non-GMO ingredients (all of Silk's beverage products are Non-GMO Project Verified). The closer any ingredient is to nature, the better it tastes and the better she feels about using it in recipes. Cathy believes that when someone starts messing with Mother Nature, ingredients tend to lose flavor and integrity.

Dairy-free, Gluten-free
Serves 4

1 can (14 ounces) regular or light coconut milk

1 teaspoon Thai red curry paste, to taste

1 tablespoon lime juice

1 tablespoon turbinado, or other unrefined sugar

1 cup Silk Unsweetened or Original soymilk, or Silk True Coconut coconut milk (plus more if needed)

6 ounces fresh green beans, cut into 1-inch pieces

12 ounces boneless, skinless chicken breast, cut into bite-sized pieces (or substitute 1 pound firm tofu, cubed)

2 plum tomatoes, cut into 4 wedges

2 tablespoons Thai fish sauce

¼ cup basil leaves, torn

4 sprigs fresh cilantro for garnish

In a wok or 4-quart stockpot, heat the coconut milk over medium-high heat. Whisk in the curry paste, lime juice, and sugar. Cook for 2 minutes, whisking frequently. Add the Silk and green beans and cook for about 8 minutes (the thinner the green beans, the faster they will cook). Add the chicken and cook an additional 5 to 7 minutes until chicken is done. If using tofu, cook until tofu is warmed through, about 5 minutes.

Add the tomato wedges, fish sauce, and basil. If curry seems too thick, additional Silk may be added. Simmer until the tomatoes are hot, 1 to 2 minutes. Garnish with cilantro and serve hot with steamed rice.

Spring Rolls

Melissa King, My Whole Food Life

Melissa writes a healthy living blog called My Whole Food Life *where she shares healthy, vegan recipes made from only whole foods. She also offers health tips and lessons on reading labels.*

Gluten-free, Vegan
Serves 6

Dipping sauce:

⅓ cup peanut butter or almond butter

¼ cup soy sauce or Bragg's Liquid Aminos

¼ cup orange juice

¼ teaspoon fresh ginger, minced

1 package rice paper rolls

1 cup carrots, julienned

1 cup cabbage, very thinly sliced

2 green onions, very thinly sliced

1 cup cucumber, julienned

1 cup firm tofu, chopped into ¼ inch cubes

¼ cup daikon, julienned

Fresh mint, basil, and/or dill, chopped

To make the dipping sauce, whisk together peanut butter, soy sauce, orange juice, and ginger; set aside.

Before rolling, dip each rice paper in warm water for 20 seconds or so until it becomes pliable. Pull it out and blot it lightly with a towel. Place vegetables and herbs in the center line of the wrap. Fold in the top and bottom and roll up. (It may take several tries to get the hang of it.) Place each finished wrap on a serving dish and serve immediately. Happy dipping!

Raw Beet Ravioli

Sonnet Lauberth

Sonnet is a certified holistic health coach, food writer, and blogger who is passionate about eating fresh foods made from scratch with organic, seasonal, and non-GMO ingredients. She is committed to educating others about healthy eating and living.

Gluten-free, Vegan
Serves 4

⅓ cup raw almonds

⅛ teaspoon sea salt, or more to taste

1 tablespoon nutritional yeast

2 tablespoons water, or more as needed

1 tablespoon fresh chives, chopped

½ cup fresh basil

1 small garlic clove

¼ teaspoon sea salt

3 tablespoons extra virgin olive oil

3 medium candy-striped beets (or any color), thinly sliced into rounds

Freshly ground black pepper to taste

To make the almond cheese, soak almonds in water for at least 1 hour, then drain. Add almonds to a food processor with salt, nutritional yeast, and 1 tablespoon of water to start. Scrape down the sides of the processor and add more water as necessary until it reaches a consistency similar to ricotta. Add the chives at the very end and pulse until incorporated.

To make the pesto oil, add the basil, garlic, and sea salt to a food processor and pulse. Add the olive oil and process until smooth, scraping down the sides as necessary.

Lay one beet slice flat, top with a little almond cheese, and lay another slice on top. Drizzle with pesto oil. Top with freshly ground black pepper and serve.

Vegetarian Feijoada

Amy Peters, Sustainable Sea Cliff Cooperative

Amy is a longtime advocate for healthy food and has worked in the health food industry for over thirty years. As a board member of her local food cooperative for the past three years, Amy has been involved in community education projects regarding food issues, including the risks of GMOs in our food supply. She has brought the Non-GMO Project's educational materials to co-op events on many occasions.

Gluten-free, Vegan
Serves 8

For the stew:

2 packages (16 ounces) tempeh, cut into ½ inch cubes

2 tablespoons mirin (Japanese cooking wine)

3 tablespoons soy sauce

6 tablespoons extra virgin olive oil

1 large yellow onion, diced

4 cloves garlic, minced

1 pinch red pepper flakes

3 teaspoons ground cumin

1 large red pepper, diced

1 large tomato, diced (or 1 small can diced tomatoes, drained)

2 bay leaves

2 tablespoons fresh thyme, chopped (or 2 teaspoons dried)

4 tablespoons fresh parsley, chopped (or 2 tablespoons dried)

1 teaspoon sea salt

1 teaspoon black pepper

2 medium sweet potatoes or yams, peeled and cut into small cubes

1 Chayote squash (optional), peeled and diced

6 cups cooked black turtle beans (about four 15-ounce cans)

2 tablespoons chipotle adobo sauce (recipe below)

Preheat oven to 350 degrees.

In a large bowl, mix the mirin, soy sauce, and 3 tablespoons olive oil. Add tempeh and toss thoroughly. Remove tempeh and place in a lasagna pan or casserole dish; cover with aluminum foil. Bake for 30 minutes. Uncover and bake for 15 minutes more, then set aside.

In a very large pan or wok, heat 3 tablespoons olive oil on medium heat and sauté onions, stirring frequently until they start to turn clear. Add garlic, red pepper flakes, and cumin, stirring with each new ingredient. Then add red pepper and sauté for about 3 minutes. Add tomatoes and sauté another 3 minutes. Stir in bay leaves, thyme, parsley, salt, and black pepper. Add sweet potatoes, chayote squash, beans, and a little of the reserved liquid from the beans.

Once the vegetables are evenly mixed, add tempeh and lower heat a little bit. Cook for about 45 minutes, partially covered, just until the potatoes and squash are tender, stirring occasionally. Add more liquid if necessary. Taste and adjust seasonings if necessary. Add chipotle adobo sauce, one tablespoon at a time, stirring and tasting until desired level of heat and smokiness is reached. Serve over brown rice.

Chipotle adobo sauce:

10 whole dried chipotle chiles, stems removed

3 cups water

⅓ cup onion, thickly sliced

2 cloves garlic, diced

5 tablespoons ketchup

4 tablespoons cider vinegar

¼ teaspoon sea salt

Mix ingredients in a saucepan and bring to a boil, then cover and simmer over very low heat for about an hour. Remove cover and simmer until liquid is reduced to about 1 cup. Cool and purée in a blender or with a hand blender. Freeze leftovers in ice cube trays and save for future use.

Beef Nachos with Fresh Guacamole and Salsa

Libby Mahoney, The Cooking Activist Company

Libby's journey began three years ago when she discovered she had an allergy to soy. Her research on soy led her to the world of GMOs and that started her campaign to transition her home away from processed, GMO-filled foods. Libby's kids, husband, family, and friends are now more aware about the dangers of GMOs. Through her business, The Cooking Activist Company, Libby educates others about food and sells non-GMO, organic, and fair trade baked goods at a local farmers market on Saturdays in Northeast Florida.

Dairy-free, Gluten-free
Serves 4

1 tablespoon extra virgin olive oil
½ yellow onion, chopped
½ green bell pepper, chopped (use a spicier pepper if desired)
2 cloves garlic, peeled and minced

1 pound lean, grass-fed ground beef
¼ cup water
¼ cup tomato sauce
Corn tortilla chips

Optional seasonings:

2 teaspoons chili powder
2 teaspoons cumin
¼ teaspoon sea salt

½ teaspoon turbinado, or other unrefined sugar
2 teaspoons paprika
2 teaspoons garlic powder

Optional toppings:

Cheddar cheese, or Monterey Jack or Colby, grated
Sour cream
Homemade guacamole (recipe follows)

Homemade salsa (recipe follows)
Romaine lettuce

Guacamole:

1 fresh avocado, pitted, peeled, and chopped

¼ tomato, diced

¼ sweet onion, minced

¼ cup fresh cilantro

1 garlic clove, peeled and minced

1 tablespoon lime juice, fresh squeezed

¼ teaspoon cumin

Sea salt and black pepper, to taste

Salsa:

½ sweet onion, chopped

1 tomato, chopped

4 ounces tomato sauce, or more to taste

2 cloves garlic, peeled and minced

1 lime, juiced

Handful of fresh cilantro, chopped

Heat the oil in a sauté pan on medium heat. Cook the onion and pepper until soft, about 5 minutes. Add the garlic and cook until fragrant, about 30 seconds. Add beef, along with desired spice mixture, to the pan. Cook until the beef is no longer pink. Pour in water and tomato sauce. Simmer on medium-low for about 10 minutes or until most of the liquid is evaporated.

To make the nachos, preheat oven to 350 degrees. Fill a large oven-safe plate or baking sheet with chips and layer the meat and shredded cheeses on top. Bake in the oven for 10–15 minutes or until cheese is fully melted and light golden. Top with desired extras and serve with fresh sour cream.

To make the guacamole, mix all ingredients together. Refrigerate in a tightly closed container until ready to serve.

To make the salsa, mix all ingredients. Add tomato sauce to get your preferred consistency. Refrigerate for at least a couple hours to let the flavors marinate.

Sweet Treats

There must be something about working hard to protect our food supply that calls for fortification from sweet treats. When we put out the call for recipe submissions, the dessert ideas came flooding in!

In our own kitchens, we both avoid wheat and refined sugar, and we have curated this section to include a lot of gluten-free choices with a focus on alternative sweeteners. Much of the white sugar sold in stores is made from sugar beets, which is a high GMO risk crop. Look for pure cane sugar instead, or better yet choose unrefined options that contain balancing trace minerals.

It's a common misperception that wheat, which is of course a common ingredient in baked goods, is all genetically engineered. Wheat has certainly been modified extensively from its original form, but there are no varieties of genetically engineering wheat approved for commercial production at this time. However, due to known contamination from GMO field trials, wheat is on our monitored crop list. We recommend that

you look for the Non-GMO Project Verified label on any wheat products that you buy.

When choosing oil for recipes, look for Non-GMO Project Verified options, or choose types that do not contain canola, cotton, or soy. Likewise, many kinds of milk (whether from cows or plants) are high GMO risk. Low-risk varieties include almond and coconut; if you use soy milk or cow's milk, be sure it is Non-GMO Project Verified. And if you bake with eggs, you'll want to make sure those chickens weren't eating GMO corn and soy! (See more about GMOs and animal products on page 102.)

Megan's kitty, Kitten Mitten, enjoys a diet of organic, non-GMO cat food.

Creamy Chia Seed Pudding

Jeffrey Smith, Institute for Responsible Technology

Jeffrey is the Executive Director of the Institute for Responsible Technology (IRT), which informs policy makers and the public about the health risks of GMOs and the serious problems associated with research, regulation, and corporate practices. He is the author of the world's bestselling book on GMOs, Seeds of Deception, *and is also the creator of the award-winning film* Genetic Roulette: The Gamble of our Lives. *Jeffrey lives with his wife in Iowa, surrounded by genetically modified soybeans and corn.*

Gluten-free, Vegan
Serves 6 to 8

1 cup chia seeds
5 tablespoons coconut sugar
¾ teaspoon cinnamon
¼ teaspoon ground cardamom
⅜ teaspoon sea salt
¼ teaspoon vanilla
4 cups coconut milk (the beverage, not canned)
    or any other type of milk

¼ cup raw extra virgin coconut oil
½ cup unsulfured Turkish dried apricots, finely
    chopped
½ cup dried currants
⅓ cup dried cherries (or other dried fruit)
1 cup toasted almonds (or other nut)

In a large mixing bowl, combine chia seeds, coconut sugar, cinnamon, cardamom, salt, and vanilla, stirring thoroughly after each addition. Add the coconut milk, followed by the coconut oil. If the oil is not liquefied, you can heat it slightly or press against side of bowl to blend. Stir in dried fruit and nuts.

The chia seeds absorb the liquid and thicken it up. Using warmed milk can speed this process up; otherwise put it in the fridge overnight to thicken. Serve in bowls or parfait glasses.

Sweet Treats

ChocoZuke Qi'a Cake

Arran Stephens, Nature's Path

Arran Stephens is the CEO and Garden Keeper at Nature's Path Organic Foods. Arran was raised on his family's organic farm, where his dad taught him to always leave the soil better than he found it. With this in mind, he and life-partner Ratana opened Nature's Path, now North America's largest organic breakfast food company, out of the back of their vegetarian restaurant in 1985. Arran has been a staunch opponent of GMO proliferation since 1990, when he learned about the harmful effects of GMOs, and is a founding board member of the Non-GMO Project.

Vegan
Makes 9 pieces

1½ cups all-purpose unbleached flour
1½ teaspoons baking soda
½ teaspoon baking powder
½ teaspoon sea salt
1½ teaspoons cinnamon
¼ teaspoon nutmeg, freshly grated
½ cup turbinado, or other unrefined sugar
½ cup light brown sugar
¾ cup canola oil

¾ cup hemp milk
1½ teaspoons pure vanilla extract
1½ teaspoons orange rind, finely grated
2 cups shredded zucchini
1 cup chocolate chips (dark chocolate for dairy-free)
½ cup shredded unsweetened coconut
¾ cup Qi'a Apple Cinnamon Cereal

Preheat the oven to 350 degrees.

Spray an 8 x 8-inch square baking pan with cooking spray. Sift flour, baking soda, baking powder, salt, cinnamon, and nutmeg into a large bowl.

In a medium bowl, whisk sugar and oil together. Whisk in hemp milk and vanilla until it emulsifies. Add liquid ingredients to dry ones and blend with a rubber spatula. Fold in the zucchini, chocolate chips, coconut, and Qi'a cereal, mixing only until combined.

Transfer batter into the baking pan, smoothing to edges. Bake for 35 to 40 minutes, or until springy to the touch and a toothpick inserted in the center comes out clean. Cool cake on a wire rack until room temperature. Cut into squares and serve.

Truly Trudy Walnut Cake

Trudy Bialic, PCC Natural Markets

Trudy Bialic is Director of Public Affairs for PCC Natural Markets, the nation's largest cooperative retail grocer. Trudy has worked on genetic engineering issues since 1994 when rBGH entered the dairy industry. She worked on the first national Campaign to Label GE foods with founder Craig Winters, ran two letter-writing campaigns at PCC generating nearly 30,000 letters, and has served on the communications and standards committees of the Non-GMO Project. She was part of a small grassroots coalition that put a GMO labeling initiative on the Washington State's 2013 ballot, and is now part of the Yes on I-522 Campaign Steering Committee.

Makes 12 slices

6 tablespoons turbinado, or other unrefined sugar, divided

1½ teaspoons cinnamon, divided

7 cups walnuts

¾ cup flour (kamut, einkorn, or unbleached white whole wheat)

1½ cups almond meal

1 teaspoon sea salt

1 cup butter or coconut oil

¾ cup turbinado, or other unrefined sugar

6 eggs

¾ cup heavy cream

½ cup whole milk yogurt

1 teaspoon vanilla extract or 1 vanilla bean, scraped

Whipped cream

Fresh sliced strawberries

Preheat oven to 350 degrees. Oil a 13 x 9-inch glass baking dish.

Combine 3 tablespoons sugar with 1 teaspoon cinnamon and sprinkle evenly over bottom of the oiled baking dish. Then pulse walnuts in a food processor until finely chopped. Set aside 2 cups. Add flour and almond meal to the remainder of the walnuts and blend until finely ground. Stir in ½ teaspoon cinnamon and salt and set aside.

In a large bowl, beat butter and ¾ cup sugar with an electric mixer until light and fluffy, about 3 minutes. Add eggs, cream, yogurt, and vanilla. Beat until ingredients are evenly mixed, about 2 minutes. Stir in the walnut/flour mixture, and then fold in 2 cups of chopped walnuts without over-mixing. Pour into baking dish and sprinkle with remaining 3 tablespoons sugar. Bake until cooked through, 50 to 55 minutes. Best if made one day before serving. Slice and serve cold with whipped cream and sliced strawberries.

Strawberry Green Thumbprint Cookies

Rachel Friedman

A West Coast transplant in Washington, DC, Rachel loves the outdoors and the beauty of agricultural systems working in concert with nature. Rachel's background is in ecology and conservation biology, but her day job deals with sustainable agriculture and food security. She tries to eat as she preaches, purchasing organic when she can and steering clear of processed food, which contains the bulk of GMO soy and corn.

Gluten-free, Vegan
Makes 24 cookies

3 tablespoons sunflower oil
¼ cup almond butter
¼ cup agave nectar
3 tablespoons unsweetened almond milk
1 teaspoon vanilla extract
1 tablespoon ground flaxseed
1 cup almond flour
⅓ cup rice flour

⅓ cup turbinado, or other unrefined sugar
2 tablespoons tapioca starch
½ teaspoon sea salt
¾ teaspoon baking powder
¾ teaspoon baking soda
¾ cup raw almonds, finely chopped
¾ cup spinach, chopped
1 cup strawberry preserves

Preheat oven to 350 degrees.

In a medium bowl, mix sunflower oil, almond butter, agave nectar, almond milk, and vanilla extract. Add flaxseed and let sit for a couple of minutes. In a large bowl, sift together almond flour, rice flour, sugar, tapioca starch, sea salt, baking powder, and baking soda. Add flax mixture, almonds, and spinach and mix until fully incorporated.

Use a tablespoon or mini ice-cream scoop to portion out 24 cookies evenly onto a Silpat or parchment paper. Bake for 8 minutes. Press center of each cookie down to make the "thumbprint," and then fill with strawberry preserves. Bake for another 4 minutes until edges start to brown. Remove from oven and cool until firm.

Sweet Ricely Cookies

Mark Squire, Good Earth Natural Foods

Mark has been an owner and manager of Good Earth Natural Foods in Fairfax, California, for over forty years. He is a founding board member of the Non-GMO Project and is one of the original proponents and authors of Measure B, the Marin County initiative that prohibited the outdoor cultivation of GMOs, which passed with 61 percent of the popular vote in 2004. Prior to his involvement with retailing, Mark managed his family's farm in North Carolina and transitioned it to organics.

Gluten-free, Vegan
Makes 12 cookies

4 cups whole grain sweet rice flour
1 cup raisins

½ cup brown sesame seeds
3 cups water

Preheat oven to 400 degrees.

Mix flour and raisins, then add water and stir to make a thick, sticky batter. Oil a cookie sheet and then sprinkle sesame seeds evenly on it. Spread the batter across cookie sheet and use your hands to pat down dough to about 1 inch thickness. Try to keep sesame distribution even.

Bake for 30 minutes, then turn sheet in oven and bake for another 15 minutes. Pull the pan out and cut the cookies into squares with a spatula. Turn them over and bake another 15 minutes. They're best eaten while still warm! These cookies are also great with diced apricots or nuts.

Super Easy Tahini Cookies

Charlene Conlin, Real Fodder Nutritional Consulting

Charlene is a Registered Holistic Nutritionist and is the owner of Real Fodder Nutritional Consulting. She first learned of GMO foods in culinary school and then again in her nutrition program and was shocked to learn that what she had been feeding her children could be so dangerous. Charlene is passionate about using whole foods as medicine and preventative care and educating others about the dangers of genetically engineered food to our health and the planet.

Dairy-free, Gluten-free
Makes 15 cookies

6 tablespoons tahini paste
1½ cups rolled oats
¾ cup honey
½ cup raw sunflower seeds

¼ teaspoon sea salt
½ cup dried cranberries (optional for a festive punch)

Preheat oven to 350 degrees.

Blend all ingredients in mixer or bowl. Place spoonfuls of the cookie dough onto a greased cookie sheet and flatten with a fork. Bake for 10 to 12 minutes or until edges are golden brown.

Chia Coconut Macaroons

Wendy Zenick, Urban Marketplace

Wendy is the owner and founder of Urban Marketplace in Ontario, Canada. After five years of trying to bring organic food to the small industrial town where she lives, she is grateful to see a growing awareness about GMOs and lots of new customers looking for healthy food choices.

Gluten-free, Vegan
Makes 25 small cookies

1 tablespoon chia seeds
1½ cups shredded unsweetened coconut
⅓ cup turbinado, or other unrefined sugar
½ cup coconut milk

6 tablespoons coconut flour
1 tablespoon golden flax meal
1 teaspoon vanilla

Preheat oven to 350 degrees.

Place chia seeds in a mixing bowl and add a tablespoon of water. Let the seeds sit for a few minutes until they congeal. Add another tablespoon of water if needed. Mix remaining ingredients with chia seeds. Use a teaspoon to scoop and form cookies. Roll between palms, place on a cookie sheet lined with parchment paper, and press down lightly to flatten the bottom slightly. Bake for 8 to 10 minutes.

Jade Matcha Panna Cotta

Shannon Beauchaine, The Republic of Tea

Shannon has been working as a designer with the food industry for many years and has always been interested in safe and conscious food sourcing. She was a member of one of the country's oldest food co-ops (Park Slope Food Co-op) for eight years until moving to the West Coast. Her viewing of a certain documentary on factory farming and the state of the food industry really solidified the importance of Non-GMO Project Verified products for her. Shannon and her fiancé are proud and excited to spread the Non-GMO word to their family, friends, and future children.

Gluten-free
Serves 8

1 cup milk, divided
2 teaspoons gelatin
2 tablespoons The Republic of Tea Matcha Stone
    Ground Tea Powder

2½ cups heavy cream
½ cup turbinado, or other unrefined sugar
1 vanilla bean

Pour ½ cup of milk into a medium bowl and sprinkle 2 teaspoons of gelatin over it. Let stand until gelatin softens, about 15 minutes.

Meanwhile, combine the tea powder, heavy cream, sugar, and the rest of the milk in a large saucepan. Cut open the vanilla bean and scrape seeds into saucepan along with the bean. Simmer over medium heat and stir until sugar has dissolved. Remove from heat, cover, and let steep for 15 minutes.

Warm cream mixture to a simmer again, this time adding the gelatin mixture and stirring until it is dissolved. Strain the mixture and divide among eight ramekins or small glasses. Chill uncovered until set (around 6 hours).

Chocolate Pudding

Gail Davis, So Delicious Dairy Free

Gail is a longtime vegan, author, blogger, and social media administrator at So Delicious Dairy Free, which offers more than 100 Non-GMO Project Verified products. Gail is passionate about sharing her love for delicious, organic, non-GMO, plant-based foods.

Gluten-free, Vegan
Serves 4

3 tablespoons turbinado, or other unrefined sugar

2 tablespoons cornstarch

⅛ teaspoon sea salt

2 cups So Delicious Dairy Free Chocolate Coconut Milk

1 tablespoon cocoa powder

1¼ cups dark chocolate chips

1½ teaspoons vanilla

In a medium bowl, whisk together sugar, cornstarch, and salt until well combined. Set aside. In a small saucepan over medium heat, combine coconut milk, cocoa powder, and chocolate chips until chips have melted into the milk, whisking continuously.

Once chips have melted, pour in the dry ingredients and continue whisking until pudding begins to boil. Turn down heat and stir until pudding thickens and coats the back of a spoon. Remove from heat, stir in vanilla, and pour into individual serving cups. Serve warm or chilled. Pudding thickens as it cools.

Sweet and Salty Brownies

Carol Kicinski, Wholesome Sweeteners

Carol is a professional recipe developer, television chef, magazine founder and editor-in-chief, freelance writer, and cookbook author. She developed this recipe for Wholesome Sweeteners, which offers a full line of Non-GMO Project Verified sweeteners.

Gluten-free
Makes 12 brownies

1¼ cups semisweet chocolate chips
1 cup softened unsalted butter
4 large eggs
1 cup Wholesome Sweeteners Organic Coconut
    Palm Sugar
6 teaspoons unsweetened cocoa powder

2 teaspoons cornstarch
½ teaspoon sea salt
1 teaspoon instant espresso powder
2 teaspoons pure vanilla extract
1½ cups salted, dry roasted peanuts, chopped

Preheat the oven to 375 degrees.

Line a 9 x 12-inch baking dish with parchment paper. Put the chocolate chips and butter in the bowl of a food processor and pulse a few times to roughly combine. Add the eggs, coconut sugar, cocoa powder, cornstarch, salt, espresso powder, and vanilla and blitz until combined. Batter is supposed to be lumpy. Spread the mixture into the prepared baking dish. Sprinkle the chopped nuts over the top and gently press into the batter.

Bake for 20 minutes or until the batter is set and it feels slightly firm to the touch. The outer edges will be a little drier than the inside. Cut into squares.

Bestest Banana Bread

Louise Shillington, Real Food Actually

Louise is a mom, lawyer, blogger, and founder of Real Food Actually and Moms Across Canada Facebook Page. After her children were born, Louise made a commitment to educating herself further so that she could make non-GMO food choices for them. She is also dedicated to helping other parents make more informed choices when buying or preparing food for their children.

Vegetarian
Makes 8 slices

1 cup brown cane sugar
¾ cup safflower or sunflower oil
1 egg
1½ cups unbleached white flour

1 teaspoon baking soda
1 teaspoon baking powder
3 to 4 ripe bananas, mashed

Preheat oven to 350 degrees.

In a large bowl, beat together sugar, oil and egg until thoroughly combined. In a separate bowl, sift together flour, baking soda and baking powder. Add dry mixture and mashed bananas to wet ingredients and mix until the batter is smooth. Pour mix into a loaf pan and bake for 1 hour or until a toothpick comes out clean. Cover the loaf with foil for the last 20 minutes or so, to prevent it from drying out.

Make sure your bananas are extremely ripe. Freezing and then defrosting can make them best for this recipe. They may seem too blackened, but once defrosted, you can snip off the tops and simply squeeze out the banana pulp.

This banana bread is best enjoyed at least one day after baking. If you can resist it, you will see how it becomes so much more moist and the top becomes tacky to the touch (a true indication it is a top-notch banana bread). It's possible to double the recipe and freeze one for a later date.

Healthy Chocolate Bites of Heaven

Zen Honeycutt, Moms Across America

As cofounder of Moms Across America along with Kathleen Hallal, Zen is committed to empowering million of moms to educate themselves about GMOs, to label GMOs, and to go GMO-free. It's a big job, though, and a girl's gotta have her chocolate at the end of the day! Zen feels good eating this healthy sweet treat, and her kids do too!

Dairy-free, Gluten-free
Makes 12 pieces

1 bag Enjoy Life semisweet chocolate mini chips
1 jar SunButter
9 Medjool dates, pitted
1 cup rolled oats (or more depending on desired consistency)

½ cup shredded coconut
½ cup sunflower seeds
¼ cup chia seeds or flaxseeds
1 teaspoon honey
1 teaspoon vanilla

Optional: coconut oil, dried strawberries, dried banana, dried figs, or nuts

In a saucepan, melt chocolate with SunButter over low heat until just melted. Put all other ingredients in a food processor; pour in chocolate and SunButter mixture and pulse until combined. Adding more oatmeal (optional for consistency) may require coconut oil for balance.

Once blended, smooth onto parchment paper on cookie sheet until about 1 inch thick. Freeze for about 2 hours. Cut with butcher knife into 1-inch squares. One piece is very rich and satisfying!

Almond Coconut Chocolate Bars

Tessa Simpson, The Domestic Diva

Tessa is a mom on a food allergy adventure, sharing her journey on a blog dedicated to wholesome, allergy-friendly living. With multiple food allergies in her household, she has learned that clean eating is the only way for her family. Non-GMO is an issue near and dear to her heart, and she strongly believes we have the right to know what is in our food.

Gluten-free, Vegan
Makes 16 bars

4 cups shredded unsweetened coconut
½ cup softened or melted coconut oil
2 to 4 tablespoons coconut nectar (or maple syrup, honey, or agave)

1½ cups dark chocolate pieces
1 tablespoon coconut oil
Roasted whole or slivered almonds (optional)

Place the coconut, coconut oil, and coconut nectar into a food processor and blend for 5 minutes. The mixture should soften and heat the coconut oil and the coconut pieces should begin to break down and move smoothly. The less time you process, the more chunky it will be. Some time is necessary so that the mixture will bind well. Taste for sweetness and add more if you like.

Line an 8 x 8-inch pan with waxed paper or parchment paper. Pour the coconut filling in and spread around evenly. If you would like to use almonds, now is the time. Press them in! Place the pan in the fridge or freezer to speed the solidifying process. Meanwhile, melt the chocolate with 1 tablespoon coconut oil.

Once the filling is solid, lift the whole chunk out by lifting the paper. Cut into desired shapes and dip each piece in the chocolate, letting the excess drip back before laying it on a Silpat, parchment, or waxed paper to solidify. You can also do these the easy way by spreading the chocolate coating right over the top of the whole pan and foregoing the dipping process!

Store in an airtight container on the counter or in the freezer. Unlike most coconut oil delicacies, these are solid at room temperature and travel well out of refrigeration in cooler temperatures.

Superfood Freezer Candy

Vani Hari, Food Babe Blog

Vani is a management consultant, food activist writer, and speaker. She started Food Babe *in April 2011 to spread information about what is really in the American food supply. She teaches people how to make the right purchasing decisions at the grocery store, how to live an organic lifestyle, and how to travel healthfully around the world.*

Gluten-free, Vegan
Makes 20 bite-size candies

1 cup almond butter	3 tablespoons raw cacao nibs
4 tablespoons coconut oil	3 tablespoons goji berries
2 tablespoons coconut palm sugar or maple syrup	½ teaspoon sea salt

Cream almond butter, coconut oil, sugar, and salt together in a bowl. Pour mixture into a small baking dish lined with parchment paper and use a spatula to spread evenly. Top with raw cacao nibs and goji berries and freeze for at least 2 hours.

Once frozen, carefully remove frozen candy by lifting ends of parchment paper. Cut candy into 1-inch squares and store in freezer separated by parchment paper.

Chocolate-Banana Melt

Alisa Gravitz, Green America

As the President and CEO of Green America (formerly Co-op America), Alisa has helped lead the national agenda to create a socially and environmentally responsible economy for nearly thirty years. Alisa cochairs Green America's newest campaign, GMO Inside, a coalition of organizations and businesses dedicated to helping all Americans know which foods contain GMOs as well as organizing concerned citizens and groups to respond to the largest GMO offenders and support state-based GMO labeling initiatives.

Gluten-free, Vegan
Serves 2

1 ripe banana
6 to 10 dark chocolate chips (or crumbled
    chocolate bar)

3 to 5 walnut halves

Cut the banana in half lengthwise and put both halves side-by-side on a glass plate or baking dish. Break up the walnut halves and press them lightly into the banana about an inch apart. Press the chocolate chips lightly into the banana, between the walnut pieces. Heat in a toaster oven for about 1 minute or until the chocolate chips are gooey.

Lemon and Rosemary Ice Cream

Fran Osborne

Since campaigning for Proposition 37 in California, Fran's household has been completely GMO-free. Originally from England, Fran's father grew all their family's vegetables when she was a child, and her first job was serving in a greengrocer. Being practicing artists, Fran's family is not wealthy, so they grow as many of their own organic vegetables and herbs as possible. They feel very lucky to have a lemon tree in their garden.

Gluten-free, Vegetarian
Serves 4

4 cups heavy whipping cream
2 cups brown sugar

Zest and juice of 4 lemons
1 sprig rosemary, washed and chopped very fine

Warm 2 cups of heavy whipping cream in a saucepan. Add the brown sugar and whisk until it has completely dissolved. Set aside until completely cool, then add the rest of the whipping cream and stir until thoroughly mixed. Add the lemon zest and lemon juice to taste and finally stir in the rosemary.

Place in a freezer-proof container and leave for 2 hours. Take out of freezer and stir thoroughly, then return to freezer. Leave for at least 5 hours and this delicious ice cream is ready to go. You can vary the amount of lemon and rosemary according to your personal taste, and ordinary cane sugar works well too. Serve with fresh fruit or lemon cake for an über lemony treat.

Yummy Pumpkin Butter

Shelby Sheehan

Shelby has two children, and when her first child was born she began an intense education about food and nutrition. She helped collect signatures to get Proposition 37 on the ballot in California, and she is dedicated to global cooperation and sustainable living.

Gluten-free, Vegan
Serves 20

1 can (15 ounces) pure pumpkin purée
1 cup peeled and grated apple (or one serving unsweetened applesauce)
½ cup firmly packed brown sugar (or substitute ⅜ cup honey or maple syrup)

¾ teaspoon pumpkin pie spice
Up to 1 cup apple juice (optional)

Combine ingredients in a heavy-duty saucepan. Bring to a boil, and then reduce heat to low. Simmer for 1½ hours, stirring occasionally. Once cooled, the pumpkin butter can be stored in a refrigerator up to two months. Each tablespoon has 15 calories and no fat.

Including the apple juice helps to caramelize the sugars and makes the butter sweeter, but is not necessary and leaving it out makes for a thicker butter.

Cooking with Non-GMO Ingredients

Substitution Chart

Food Category	High GMO Risk Ingredients	Non-GMO Substitutions
Alternative Dairy Beverages	Soy milk	Low-Risk: Almond milk, coconut milk, hazelnut milk Non-GMO Project Verified soy milk or rice milk
Alternative Meat Products	Tofu, tempeh, "alternative" meats	Non-GMO Project Verified tofu, tempeh, "alternative" meats
Baking Agents	Baking powder, cornstarch	Low-Risk baking powder substitute: ¼ cup baking soda ½ cup cream of tartar ¼ cup arrowroot powder Low-Risk cornstarch substitute: arrowroot powder
Beans and Legumes	Edamame, soybeans	Low-Risk: All beans and legumes except soy (black beans, cannellini beans, split peas, lentils, etc.) Non-GMO Project Verified edamame and soybeans
Dairy and Eggs	Milk, butter, cheese, eggs	Low-Risk: Non-dairy alternatives (see above) Non-GMO Project Verified milk, butter, cheese, and eggs

Flavor Enhancers	Nutritional yeast, tamari, soy sauce	Non-GMO Project Verified nutritional yeast, tamari, and soy sauce
Fruit	Papaya (from Hawaii)	Low-Risk: All fruit except papaya from Hawaii Certified Organic papaya, or papaya not from Hawaii
Grains and Flours	Cornmeal/flour, soy flour, flour blends containing corn or soy; breads and cereals containing corn, soy and/or canola	Low-Risk: All grains and flours not containing corn or soy (can use millet as a replacement for cornmeal) Non-GMO Project Verified cornmeal/flour and soy flour; Non-GMO Project Verified breads and cereals
Meat and Fish	Chicken, beef, pork, lamb, and fish	Low Risk: Wild-caught fish Non-GMO Project Verified meat
Oils and Fats	Oils and oil blends derived from corn, canola, and/or soy; margarine, butter, lard	Low-Risk: For high-temperature cooking try coconut oil, sunflower oil, or safflower oil. For low-temperature cooking use extra virgin olive oil. Non-GMO Project Verified butter or lard
Sauces, Soups, and Stocks	Sauces, soups, and stocks containing canola oil, corn-based ingredients, sugar, and soy-based flavorings	Low-Risk: homemade versions not containing canola, soy, or corn ingredients Non-GMO Project Verified sauces, soups, and stocks

Cooking with Non-GMO Ingredients

Sugars and Sweeteners	White sugar (often is from high GMO risk beet sugar), corn syrup, artificial maple syrup (may contain corn syrup), aspartame, sucrose, honey	Low-Risk: cane sugar, coconut sugar, pure maple syrup, agave Non-GMO Project Verified honey
Vegetables	Sweet corn, crookneck squash, zucchini	Low-Risk: All other vegetables Non-GMO Project Verified sweet corn, crookneck squash, zucchini

Conversion Charts
Metric and Imperial Conversions
(These conversions are rounded for convenience)

Ingredient	Cups/Tablespoons/Teaspoons	Ounces	Grams/Milliliters
Butter	1 cup=16 tablespoons= 2 sticks	8 ounces	230 grams
Cream cheese	1 tablespoon	0.5 ounce	14.5 grams
Cornstarch	1 tablespoon	0.3 ounce	8 grams
Flour, all-purpose	1 cup/1 tablespoon	4.5 ounces/0.3 ounce	125 grams/8 grams
Flour, whole wheat	1 cup	4 ounces	120 grams
Fruit, dried	1 cup	4 ounces	120 grams
Fruits, chopped	1 cup	5 to 7 ounces	145 to 200 grams
Fruits, puréed	1 cup	8.5 ounces	245 grams
Honey, maple syrup, or corn syrup	1 tablespoon	.75 ounce	20 grams
Liquids: cream, milk, water, or juice	1 cup	8 fluid ounces	240 milliliters
Oats	1 cup	5.5 ounces	150 grams
Salt	1 teaspoon	0.2 ounce	6 grams
Spices: cinnamon, cloves, ginger, or nutmeg (ground)	1 teaspoon	0.2 ounce	5 milliliters
Sugar, brown, firmly packed	1 cup	7 ounces	200 grams
Sugar, white	1 cup/1 tablespoon	7 ounces/0.5 ounce	200 grams/12.5 grams
Vanilla extract	1 teaspoon	0.2 ounce	4 grams

Oven Temperatures

Fahrenheit	Celsius	Gas Mark
225°	110°	$1/4$
250°	120°	$1/2$
275°	140°	1
300°	150°	2
325°	160°	3
350°	180°	4
375°	190°	5
400°	200°	6
425°	220°	7
450°	230°	8

Acknowledgments

Thank you to the amazing Non-GMO Project Team who held down the fort while we endeavored to pull this cookbook together during a time of record growth and activity in the office. Special thanks to Isabel VanDerslice who organized documents, managed communications with contributors, edited recipes, and made many of the dishes featured in these pages. Thank you also to Isaac Bonnell, whose eagle-eye editing skills provided great reassurance throughout the process. And thank you to Chris, Dede, and Arielle for working so passionately every day for the non-GMO cause and for being so fun and pleasant while doing it!

Our sincere gratitude goes to Abigail Gehring at Skyhorse Publishing for inviting us to do this project and for coming out to Bellingham and taking such beautiful photos along with her equally talented husband, Tim Lawrence.

Megan Westgate: I am so thankful to my parents for raising me with an appreciation for gardening, good food, and the sanctity of the natural world. To Noah, my husband, best friend, and divine playmate—I offer my very deepest gratitude. For the countless salads and other nourishing treats you have brought to me during the long nights and weekends of work it has taken to build the Non-GMO Project; for all of the times you have cajoled me into stepping away from the computer to enjoy a proper meal at the table, or to come outside to breathe the fresh air. For the past six years you have kept the garden growing and the good food flowing, providing a constant reminder of why I really do this work. We have so much to protect and to be grateful for.

Courtney Pineau: I would like to give thanks to my family for teaching me to cook and garden with passion and creativity. We have shared so many fantastic meals together! To my daughter and shining star, Sophia—you truly are my muse. Thank you for infusing my life with your contagious energy. Your presence reminds me on a daily basis why this work is so important. To my beloved husband and soul's mate, Jeff—my sincere gratitude for walking this path with me. There is not a day that goes by that I don't give thanks for having the opportunity to share this life with you.

INDEX